IMPERFECT

A Raw Memoir and Guided
Journal for the Broken, the
Brave, and the Ever-Evolving

KAT FLORIDIA

DEDICATION

My book is for those who feel imperfect yet continue to search for meaning in a world that often feels overwhelming. If you feel the world surrounds you with limitations and obstacles that are beyond comprehension, may you find strength and courage in your journey.

To my father and my sister Samantha: I hope to continue making you both proud.

To the WNBA player whose confidence and perseverance reignited my own: Thank you for reminding me what it means to live with purpose and vitality.

INTRODUCTION

This book is a labor of my truth. It is not to seek sympathy; it is a testament of survival. It's not polished or perfect, but it's real. It's to serve as a reminder that imperfection is not a weakness but a powerful thread that connects us all as human beings. Whether you were born imperfect, like me, or became imperfect due to a tragic situation, your story holds immense value. We all face many obstacles. We know how cruel the world can be, especially when it holds us to unattainable standards. But within each of us lies a light waiting to be uncovered. My story is for anyone who has ever felt unseen, unheard, or underestimated. It's not just for those with physical disabilities, but for every soul who has felt or carries the weight of being different. My hope is to inspire you to embrace your uniqueness, ignite your inner strength, and shape the most empowered version of yourself.

Those who believe in God trust that each of us is here for a purpose and everything happens for a reason. Still, many of us share the unanswered question: "Why did God choose whom he did to be imperfect?" Don't worry, this book won't preach to you. It's a story of a physically disabled, reserved, timid girl, crippled with anxiety, trying to make sense of a world that rarely makes room for her. Through pain, doubt, and small moments of courage, I've searched for meaning, purpose, and a reason to keep going.

Now, who am I, and why would you want to read my book? I don't have all the answers. What I do have are raw, real, life-altering personal experiences that will remind you that you are not alone. The imperfect you has been made to feel like a nobody. It's time to alter that narrative. We are not invisible. We are all important, irrespective of our imperfections.

My story is for those who don't have the strength to speak out, but are tired of being judged, stared at, passed over, told you *cannot* and *will not* because you are imperfect. For those whose dreams and aspirations may have been thwarted because others in this world believe they have the power to limit you. I have been broken, humiliated, and judged my whole life, but I'm tired of being silenced.

While you are reading about my journey, I invite you to explore your own. You will find an "Ink Your Thoughts" section at the end of each chapter. These dedicated pages are an invitation to pause, turn inward, and explore your insights. The questions are designed to guide your introspection and help uncover experiences that have shaped your own personal journey.

To cite the insightful prose of George Elliot: "It is never too late to be what you might have been."

HER

This message is intended for anyone who has ever drawn strength from a public figure and wishes they could thank them. Someone whose words, actions or presence gave you the courage to keep going when life felt overwhelming. We all know life doesn't come without hardships; the path is often littered with setbacks, heartbreaks, and moments that test you. However, within those trials and tribulations lies a hidden gift: the opportunity to discover a new kind of light. Not the one that simply illuminates your path, but the one that radiates from within, forged by resilience and shaped by every challenge you have overcome. The light that will allow you to shine brighter than you ever imagined.

Some of you may be wondering about the unnamed WNBA player mentioned in my dedication. Though her identity remains private, her influence on my life has been transformative. She is the reason this book exists, and her influence runs through every page. For the longest time, I moved through life following the script of adulthood, going through the motions and doing what was expected, yet I wasn't truly living. She inspired me to finally take control of my life, strive for more, and share my story. It only feels right to dedicate a piece of my book to her. Every individual is worthy of their own flowers, which is why she deserves the appropriate recognition.

I am grateful to this WNBA player, who we will henceforth refer to as "HER." The light at the end of my tunnel, my greatest inspiration, and the person I strive to be. I wouldn't have put pen to paper if it were not for HER awakening in me a newfound sense of vitality.

HER is just one of many public figures who use their platforms to influence opportunities for those who are working toward a better tomorrow. She reminds me to foster and embody my own self-confidence. My upbringing didn't consist of strong women who were inspirational or empowering, but rather those who would tear me down. My ability to accept myself and all my imperfections has been gained by observing women like HER.

I'm still trying to find my purpose in life—crazy, right? Is it weird that more than a quarter of my life is complete and I still fear the world? Scars still define me. I am stronger and smarter, so shouldn't I know better? I guess it's just another funny way the world reminds you that you are human. Scars are everlasting reminders of our past. The past was real and wounds *can* heal, but it doesn't mean you *will* heal.

As I reflect on my childhood, I wish I had grown up with someone like HER. I get the impression she would have been the anchor of a best friend I needed to get me through the tough times. You know, the type of ride-or-die friend we all yearn for. The kind of person who doesn't just show up when things are good, but stays and holds you up when you can't stand on your own. The one who's with you until the wheels fall off. You can tell them anything and they will never judge you.

If you don't have someone already, I hope you find someone like HER to look up to. The person who gives you the courage and confidence to persevere. The person who motivates you to live with greater intention, act with greater compassion, cultivate self-love, and make positive contributions to society. The person who encourages you to find and use your voice or, at the very least, makes you feel like you have discovered it.

Like many of us, HER speaks minimally of her childhood and upbringing. She tends to be more reserved and chooses to keep her life private. (I did too, until I had this crazy idea to write a book!) The tenacity of her motivates me to better myself each day. I feel encouraged to take care of my mind and body, find peace and self-love, stay humble and reach my hand out to those in need, and pause and think about how I want to be remembered.

When I still encounter moments of self-doubt or lack of self-worth or self-love, I look to HER for guidance. Whether it be watching her games on TV or in the stands, or how she presents herself to the media, it reminds me not to allow old shadows of the past darken my light. It's like someone whispering in my ear, "Kat, look in the mirror and see all that you've accomplished." A reminder that nothing is given, it's only earned.

During moments of weakness, I close my eyes and remind myself the imperfect me has achieved more than I ever could have imagined:

I've worked multiple jobs and saved every penny to establish my own financial security.

I don't need an elevator because I can confidently use the stairs—and prefer to.

I have a she shed, I climb ladders, use chainsaws, drive my John Deere, and practice carpentry.

I walk faster than most *normal* people.

I exercise, lift weights, and walk two crazy dogs by myself.

I am strong as hell! When someone tells me, "You can't," I respond, "Watch me!"

I know how far I've come, yet some days I open my eyes and question why I feel so alone. Why do I believe I have so much more to prove and accomplish? It's because imperfect individuals are convinced we have more to prove, and everything we do never seems to be enough.

I recently came across a video of HER on social media where she expressed how she needed a win in her life. The initial thought that crossed my mind was, "Wow, what a powerful expression!" It's easy for outsiders to look at individuals like HER and assume she is always winning in life with all she has achieved in her sport. It just illustrates the significance of perception. Anyone can appear "perfect" from the outside, yet not feel triumphant on the inside.

Here creeps in the thoughts of the imperfect you . . .

We all aim for victories, whether they're big or small, to keep ourselves motivated. Life is hard. We want to understand the sky is the limit with the right work ethic. We all desire to experience the sensation of accomplishment once our goals have been achieved. The responsibility for identifying and determining one's own personal achievement lies within. It may not be as obvious as winning a championship or getting a promotion; it could be something much more profound.

We all experience those moments when we long for a win. My win is still unknown. It could be meeting HER one day, or publishing a successful book that resonates with others. Only I will know that gratifying feeling when that moment happens. *I'm still waiting for my win in life.*

Each day, I continue my story with an ounce of hope to emerge stronger, wiser, and better than I have ever been. With faith, I believe each step, detour, and decision I make are aligned with a greater purpose. I have journeyed through my own hell and braved life's roughest storms to realize I have to be my own reason to smile. Life can be trying and far from ideal; mine is a testament to that truth. At its core, my story is about embracing persistence, resilience, and determination. I strive to dig deep within myself, defying every adversity in an unbreakable quest to create my best self.

Like my father always says, "God, gives challenges to those He knows have the strength to handle them." I'm finding a lesson within each obstacle I have endured. I aim to find purpose in every experience by reconnecting with my faith and regaining self-confidence through the influence of women like HER. The inspiration she has given me has been a catalyst in my self-discovery, leading me to unveil and embrace my true authentic self. Is this me finally coming out the other side? Am I finding my light at the end of the tunnel?

To all those who consider themselves imperfect, I hope you find some peace and hope reading my life's journey. My story is not going to provide all of the answers or solutions. It is not a self-help book. Yet, I will let you determine if my words are the guidance you need to inspire your walk toward acceptance. I apologize if I disappoint you. I'm still struggling to accept my imperfect self, and my story is still being written. I acknowledge that I have grown and overcome hurdles I never imagined were achievable. However, I'm still seeking a deeper understanding of God's direction with respect to how it aligns with my inner peace and happiness.

If you learn anything from my story, I hope it's to not let the stares, the pointing, and the debilitating comments define or destroy you, like I did for a quarter of my life. Use your scars and agony to remind yourself that you are a survivor and a fighter. My hope is that you will find the will to be stronger than I was, because it was a hard lesson to learn alone.

The first step is to accept yourself before seeking acceptance from those around you. Other people's expectations do not determine your worth. Take pride in yourself and embrace your quiet strengths. Who you are today is a result of your endurance and perseverance.

My manifestation is sent into the universe with the hope of meeting HER one day. In God's plan, that still may be a story waiting to be written.

*Hang in there,
the imperfect you.
The rest of your story
is still unfolding.*

Use the space below to let your thoughts flow freely.

Is there someone you aspire to meet? Why?

What qualities or achievements of this person inspire you?

What inspires you in your daily life?

Think about moments, people or experiences that spark your motivation.

What do you like about yourself today?

Do you have imperfections that you feel define you in either a positive or negative way?

MY STORY BEGINS

Allow me to bring you back in time to 1992, when this disabled, reserved girl, crippled with anxiety, was born in Moscow, Russia. Now, why do I keep identifying myself as either "handicapped," "disabled," or "crippled"? It's because society seems to think it's okay to call me or judge me based on those three little words, so it's only appropriate I refer to myself the same way, don't you think? Please do not take offense, as I am only directing these words toward myself.

Life handed me a challenge the moment I took my first breath. My birth parents couldn't understand or accept that I wasn't whole. Therefore, in the earliest chapter of my life, they made the heartless decision to leave me in an orphanage. Of course, I was too young to remember that moment, but its impact echoed throughout the years. That abandonment built the foundation of who I am and shaped my ongoing journey of resilience, hope, and the quiet strength of survival. I was born with congenital lower limb deficiency, due to amniotic band syndrome (ABS). ABS is a rare condition where the amniotic bands form inside the amniotic sac. These bands constricted the growth of both my legs. In many countries in 1992, access to specialized resources and support networks were both scarce and fragmented for lower limb deficiencies.

I cannot help but wonder, if I wasn't born imperfect, would my biological parents have kept me? Did they keep my older sister who was listed in my documents? Am I really Russian? My birth certificate indicates my biological father's nationality is Azerbaijanian and my mother's nationality is Tartar? *My mind can only wonder.*

It only took eighteen months for a willing mother and her best friend to travel across the world from the state of Massachusetts to Moscow. This willing mother saw past my imperfections and knew there were resources to give me a better future in the United States.

While writing my memoir, I was curious about what convinced my saving grace of a mother to adopt me. When I asked her, she explained there was something about one photo at the adoption agency that moved her deeply. She stated it felt like she was looking at a reflection of herself.

In all honesty, I really wasn't supposed to be here as part of this family. My father had drawn a firm line: no more children. The foster home my parents created was stretched to its limits, and he was already struggling with the emotional weight of being a guardian to so many. A role he never truly signed up for. It was my mother's dream, not his. But my mother . . . she's a force of nature. Without telling anyone, she boarded a plane to Russia and when she returned, she didn't just bring back a child, she brought back me. An imperfect child with no legs. That shook the whole family. There was tension. Disbelief. The house was already bursting at the seams, and now there was one more mouth to feed. My father and siblings were upset. Even though I was young, I felt a disconnect between them and me. However, somehow, through all that chaos, I found a home. A place in a story I wasn't supposed to be part of. That's why, even now, I carry this quiet gratitude, because against all odds, I was chosen.

It's possible my parents were sent from heaven to rescue me from the harms of the unknown. However, I want to emphasize that my life was not exactly perfect. My parents are the kind of people who have big hearts and big dreams, but are *broke as hell*. For many years, my mother opened our home to more than 100 foster children, providing support as they came and went. She cared for so many that she and my dad won the Best Foster Parents of the Year Award. Although it was a source of income for our home, it was more detrimental for my two biological and three adopted sisters who came before me. In conversations we discovered we didn't receive the individual attention, love, or care we craved. Our father never relinquished his aspiration to become a professional golfer. That ambition impaired his judgement, prompting him to favor his passion for the sport over practical responsibilities like a well-paid, nine-to-five, pensioned job.

You're probably thinking, "Wow, you have a big family! You must have had a lot of support surrounding you and did everything together." Wrong! Despite being part of a large family, I never felt more alone or different. To put it succinctly, I was the black sheep of the family. From a young age, I realized my path in life wouldn't be easy, and my success would demand ten times the effort of the average person. There is a sixteen-year age gap between my oldest sister and me, so almost a generational divide. I am the youngest, the most forgotten, and don't forget, *I'm imperfectly different.*

My sisters were everything I dreamed of being. They were beautiful, smart, athletic, and effortlessly popular. From cheerleading and Pop Warner football to track meets and school events, they were always in the spotlight. Boys tripped over themselves just to get their attention. They were the kind of girls who were always invited to every party and in the middle of all the action, even when it meant getting involved in things they probably shouldn't have been. They had a social circle that seemed endless. A list of friends they could call at any time to make plans, go out, or just hang out.

Then there was the imperfect me . . . where did I fit in? At a young age, I learned the art of suffering in silence and internalizing it. *Ah, the art of perception and hiding behind a social mask.* People would perceive me as a happy, optimistic, loving individual because that's what society expects to see. Society stresses either good or bad, happy or sad, healthy or sick, strong or weak. Society is not interested in the complete context of an individual's life or personal struggles.

What people never realize is that imperfect individuals feel your stares, see your pointing, hear your comments, and avoid your touch. To date, society has never grasped or understood the magnitude of these actions, which take a small piece of us. We *choose* to suffer in silence and display a fake smile, which enables others to perceive their actions as acceptable.

The most challenging aspect of growing up was the absence of other imperfect individuals around me. I stood out like a sore thumb in school. It gave students, teachers, staff, and parents something to stop and stare at. In addition, it gave them all permission to treat me differently, although I didn't seek or welcome it.

"Kat, do you need to take the elevator? We know the stairs must be difficult for you."

"Kat, do you need extra time to get to your next class?"

"Oh Kat, you're a little late, but I know it is hard for you to get around."

I was two minutes behind the bell because I had to use the girl's room, but believe whatever you want.

"Now Kat, Mr. Archer will be your personal assist to help you exit the building during fire drills."

There are only two floors. I don't need assistance.

"Kat, are you able to participate in all gym activities? Please do not feel obligated to participate in activities that you are unable to do."

Like, damn . . . STOP IT! I wanted to scream all the time. The adults were worse than my classmates. Did adults not understand that coddling me influenced the students' behavior around me? I should be the one who dictates my limitations, and I honestly never learned that until I got older.

On top of already being disabled, I had myopia (nearsightedness), so I had to add spectacles to my ever-glamorous look. In elementary school reading comprehension was another hurdle for me, and I was falling behind in my grade level. That ultimately got me placed into special education classes, which is a common destination for imperfect students. Students enrolled in special ed are often ridiculed, bullied, and even more coddled.

Oh, just what I need—more unnecessary coddling!

It felt like I couldn't win. I always thought, *God, why am I being set up to fail in life?* I was already born imperfect. Now I must deal with reading and vision challenges? It all seemed like a nightmare I would never wake up from. At such a young age, what was I supposed to do? The truth is, I just had to accept the hand I was dealt. My lack of self-confidence caused me to be more reserved and closed off. I knew I was different, which made it hard to make friends. Other mothers would always smile and be cordial, but I saw their judgmental eyes, skeptical expressions, their arms crossed, doubting my capabilities to have a *normal* playdate with their son or daughter at the park.

Mothers would whisper, "Is that Floridia's kid? Is she going to be okay playing with so-and-so?"

"Be careful playing with Kat because she can't run around too much and she could get hurt."

"Kat, do you think it's a good idea for you to use the monkey bars?"

"Kat, are you sure you can climb up the ladder to the slide? Should I pick you up?"

I remember distinctly this one episode where a mom's question provoked their child to ask, "Mom, why does Kat walk like that? What is wrong with her?"

"Kat is different. She is *special.* She may not be able to run, climb, and play like you and your friends do," the mother responded.

Another classic example of me being ostracized. They thought their comments were harmless, yet in reality, they were harmful.

Imperfect individuals are both sensitive and professional observers who are always aware of their surroundings. Our secret weapon is supersonic hearing, which allows us to hear everything, even if you think we don't. I may have been young, but I wasn't stupid.

What was I supposed to do?

Cry?

Scream?

Talk back?

Why would I want to give other parents the satisfaction?

So what did I do? I smiled and continued to play as best as I could, the best I knew how.

The world isn't fair. As an imperfect individual, it feels like you can never win, right? Well, you're damn right! That's how society made me feel.

I see you, I hear you, and I feel you.

We are all in this together, you are not alone. When *you* feel pain, *I* feel pain. Regardless of how many discrimination laws are in place to protect us, imperfect individuals will never be fully recognized for anything beyond their imperfections because of those who prefer to judge a book by its cover.

As a young kid, I only had one genuine friend named Emma. She lived down the street, and we played on the same soccer team.

Wait . . . hold on. *You* played soccer?

I thought you were handicapped!

How did this happen?

How was it allowed?

How did the other parents react?

Let me explain.

Even with everyone doubting me at such a young age, I still wanted to try and be a kid. To be honest, I can't recall exactly how or why I first got into soccer. What I do remember is the thrill of competition. The drive to push myself and test my limits. That passion for the competitive nature of sports quickly grew into a love for both soccer and basketball, where I found purpose and identity in the challenges of being an athlete.

Emma's dad always made sure I had playing time, not out of obligation, but because he believed I belonged on the field. There was something gentle in the way Emma and her parents accepted me, as if they saw past everything the world often couldn't and simply welcomed who I was. They saw the true me, beyond being disabled. Emma's parents gave us space to be ourselves, never hovering, never intruding. Their home was always a place of ease. They trusted us to come to them if we needed anything, and that trust gave us freedom. Even as Emma's world shifted and popularity found her with new friendships, she always made sure I was included. Her loyalty was quiet but unwavering. In a world that often made me feel like I didn't quite fit, Emma reminded me that I did.

One of Emma's sleepover birthday parties remains one of my most cherished memories, not just for the laughter and late-night whispers, but for the sense of safety I felt in an environment that made me feel exposed.

Emma was the only friend I trusted enough to see me without my prosthetics. I removed them before bed or a shower, but doing so around others filled me with dread. That night I hesitated, unsure if I could go through with it. To help me feel more comfortable, Emma's mother stepped in with a grace I'll never forget. She gathered the girls together and spoke with gentle authority, explaining my prosthetics in simple, compassionate terms. She made it clear that unkindness would not be tolerated. It helped a little, but it was still nerve-racking. I still got those stares, but they were different this time. They came from curiosity, not cruelty, and that shift, subtle as it was, meant everything.

Emma's mom had endearing strength and a natural gift for guiding others. Her influence shaped how the other girls responded to me. Her positivity stood in stark contrast to the negative assumptions I frequently faced from other adults, who perceived me as helpless and incapable. Young kids are influenced by the adults around them, and Emma's mom never treated me any different than the other girls. That night, during the sleepover, I wasn't defined by my prosthetics. I was simply part of the group. And for the first time, I felt like I belonged.

In this rare instance I realized: *Okay, I am an imperfect girl, but there are people in this world that can see past my imperfections and treat me like everyone should be treated.*

Even though I genuinely appreciated everything Emma's mother did for me on this occasion and many others, the harsh reality remains that I will eternally be a handicapped, imperfect girl. From grade school to my college years, I would wear long pants year-round—yes, even through the sweltering summers—just to hide my prosthetics. It never really mattered though, because my limp is always the first thing people notice when I walk into a room, and it still feels like that's all they see.

The world always seems to find a cruel way to remind me I am *imperfectly unique.* My infamous limp instantly invites people to ask, "Is your foot okay?" or "Is your knee okay?" They ask with a tilt of their head, a look of concern, even a smile. Harmless, right? People are probably just curious or concerned, but every time, I feel a little jolt. Not because they are necessarily rude, but because it reminds me how quickly society notices when something is different. I inevitably offer a polite smile and try to brush it off, even though part of me wants to ask why they felt the need to ask anything at all. I take their question as criticism. We are taught to be kind, to be considerate, yet curiosity often overrides compassion. In these moments, I can't help but feel like I'm being reduced to a single detail—a limp—rather than seen as a person.

I tried out all sorts of limp rationales . . .

"Oh, I just tripped and fell the other day, but I am fine."

"Oh, I twisted my ankle."

"Oh, I got hurt in gym class."

"Oh, I hurt my knee in a soccer game."

Ultimately, I opted for a sports injury response, as it was the easiest and most plausible explanation for me to give to others.

Sadly, my truth is that deep within I have always longed to not be myself. As a human being I have felt sad, desperate, lost, and unloved. It dawned on me that to survive in this world, I needed to pretend to be someone who was less fragile to fit into the societal norm. I figured it was easier to let the world define me than to fight an unwinnable uphill battle.

I often find myself wondering what kind of athlete I might have been if I had not been born imperfect. Could I have made the varsity team in high school or even competed at the collegiate level? Would I have drawn more attention from boys? Might I have built more meaningful friendships with girls who I could hang out with and call in times of need? Would I have been more of an extrovert who was more confident in social circles? My mind ponders these questions, imagining the alternative life I might have lived.

To the Imperfect You:

Does it feel fair that we must suffer in silence? Are you fed up with fantasizing about and pretending to be someone else? Have you had enough of apologizing and making excuses for your inabilities? I bet you have. There are a lot of "normal" individuals who don't put in the time or effort, yet they are recognized as mentally and physically more able. I am certain that if you ask any imperfect individual, you will discover they can accomplish all things they put their mind to.

The unfortunate reality is that imperfect individuals will continue to struggle to gain acceptance from society as long as there are individuals who choose to be ignorant. If viewpoints are not changed, we will never be recognized for anything more than our imperfect selves. Together, it is imperative that we become more aware of our own humanity and the world we shape through our collective daily actions. This is why I am sharing my story. It's essential that no one else spends more than a quarter of their life striving to be someone other than their true imperfect selves.

Because damn . . . it's exhausting! Yeah, it's exhausting to constantly have to be the bigger person and pretend other people's actions don't have an impact on you. It's exhausting to remind yourself each morning that it's not necessary to hide behind a fake façade instead of just embracing your true self. It's exhausting to constantly think you have to pose as someone you're not just to feel accepted in society. I strive to harmonize these sentiments as I journey toward living as my true authentic self. *I'm a work in progress.*

What I can say is my resilience can be attributed to the pain and adversity of being different over the years. The lifelong stares, pointing, and comments have only motivated me to become better and stronger than I ever could've imagined. I'm sorry to all those bullies who thought I'd allow their immaturity to break me. Your scars will forever be engraved in me. They will serve as essential reminders that I am a survivor.

You, yes you, are a survivor. The imperfect you is a fighter!

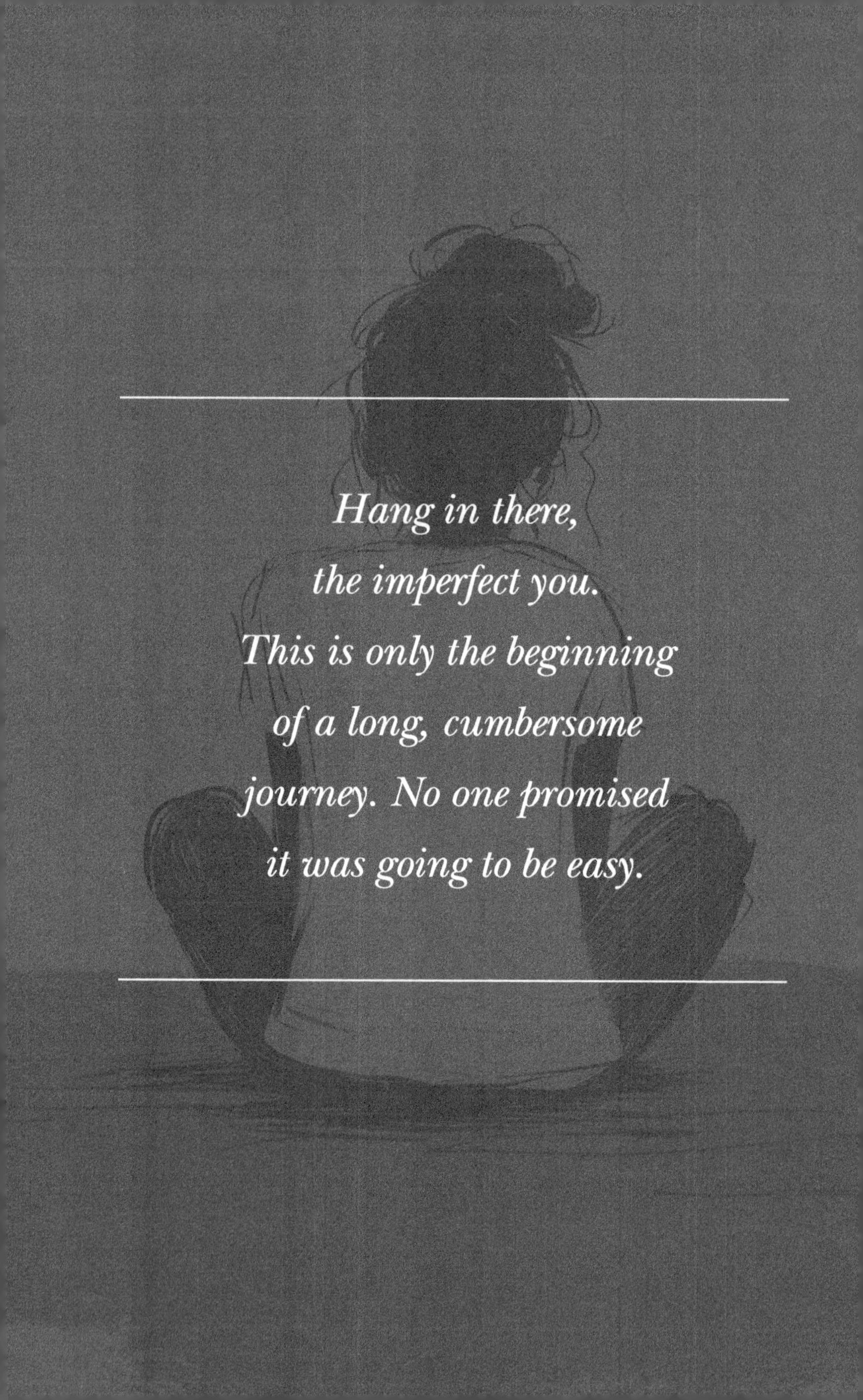

*Hang in there,
the imperfect you.
This is only the beginning
of a long, cumbersome
journey. No one promised
it was going to be easy.*

Use the space below to let your thoughts flow freely.

Do you have a childhood memory that shaped you into who you are today?

It can be positive or negative. How did you change your thought process?

Do you have someone in your life, like my Emma, who truly sees you for who you are?

Describe your relationship with this person. How do they support you and how does it feel to be understood by them?

What tends to exhaust you emotionally, mentally, physically?

Is it a specific situation, person, or pattern? How do you cope with your exhaustion?

MY CONSTANT

Is there someone in your life who has been your constant? Is this one person your rock and confidant? Have they been your day one, standing by you through the thick and thin? Does this person remain by your side through the ups and downs, never faltering, always striving to lift your spirits and make you smile? For me, this person is my dad. He is my stabilizing force in life and encompasses every quality above. He has a heart of gold and a spirit rooted in faith. He is the kind of man who will give you the shirt off his back and his last dollar without hesitation. His character is shaped by his devotion to God. Among the many values he has instilled in me, the most significant is the belief in the power of giving and that what you give comes back tenfold.

Over the years, I have cultivated a habit of giving, and my love language is centered around service. It's through acts of service that others also win me over. We've all heard the saying, "Actions speak louder than words." But while actions speak for themselves, I realized that my desire to hear my father's affirmations was a missing element in life. I yearned to hear those six little words every daughter wants to hear, "Peanut, I am proud of you." My dad illustrated his worth through his actions, but he had difficulty expressing emotions such as "I love you" or "I'm proud of you." His philosophy was I already knew his love and pride for me, yet I didn't. I waited and hoped he would say something, anything, to make me feel seen, but words weren't his way. He constantly made me feel like those words had to be earned, which motivated me to dedicate my entire life to proving myself to him and exemplifying my worth.

While I was growing up, my dad's life revolved around two things: golf and his job as a salesman. His dedication to both meant he was often away, sometimes only home a couple of times a week. I remember watching the clock, hoping he would walk through the door, but mostly he was on the road, chasing the dollar that never materialized.

Still, despite his frequent absences, I could count on him for the moments that truly mattered when he was home. He never missed a soccer game if he was in town, even though I spent most of my time being a dedicated benchwarmer. He would be there in the stands, cheering me on as if I were the star player. When I joined the school drama club, he showed up for every performance, whether I had just a single line or was working behind the scenes because my teacher didn't think I was cut out for acting.

My dad viewed every role I played as equally important, so he didn't care what my role was on the field or during drama performances. His goal was to give me the grace that I was incapable of giving myself. He repeatedly made me feel like I belonged, despite others tormenting me into thinking I didn't. He understood the significance of all the roles I played that were not fully appreciated by others. For a drama performance to be successful, it is necessary for someone to be responsible for managing the scenery. A team needs bench players to relieve their teammates, even if it's only for a few minutes. His intention was for me to comprehend that everything I accomplished was valuable, even if others thought it was trivial. He acknowledged my purpose. He made me feel visible. He encouraged me to stay involved and to have faith in his commitment to show up for me.

My dad recently told me that one of his cherished memories is from when I was six years old, lacing up my tiny running shoes for the weekly Wednesday night track club. I competed in a fifty-yard dash and, of course, I was about ten or twenty yards behind the other kids. But my dad told me it never discouraged me. He remembers the roar of the crowd urging me forward as I sprinted with everything I had. As I crossed the finish line, Mr. Ryan, a well-known TV personality, reached out with a high-five and said with enthusiasm, "You are amazing!" My dad picked me up and twirled me around because I never quit. The crowd was captivated by my grit, fueled by my unwavering determination and heart, and I was unexpectedly given an additional third-place ribbon.

A pivotal triumph like this should have been more enjoyable to me. I realize that when I was younger, I felt life was always moving forward and I didn't take the time to appreciate the everyday delights. Looking back, I wish I had slowed down, lived more fully in uncomplicated moments and genuinely absorbed the experiences that now feel so precious. Growing up, I never really appreciated those fleeting, tender moments because I was too consumed by how others perceived me. I allowed society's perception of me to take precedence over everything.

I relinquished my achievements and joy to society.

Despite my perspective on society, my dad consistently found ways to divert my focus onto my heart and helped me see beyond my imperfections. My dad always gave me the look that signified he saw the true me. Even when words weren't necessary (or so he thought), he validated my pain and sorrow. He was, and is, my biggest cheerleader and made me feel more than—not less than. I habitually felt less than because my mind was consumed by others' ignorance. My dad's guidance was centered around encouraging me to thrive and not to just survive.

Throughout my childhood, my dad quietly shaped the fundamental parts of my identity. Many around me share that my dad has been my most loyal and devoted supporter. My dad never saw me as flawed or imperfect. He recognized that life could present challenges for me, but he was determined that they would never define me or hinder my success. He wanted me to be secure in myself and to never give weight to the voices of doubt around me. Perhaps this is why my childhood lacked physical affection, a need I only came to understand later. His intention was to instill strength in me, but in hindsight, embodying resilience was not the only thing I needed. My dad is not perfect—no one is. He invested his time and effort into preparing me for the world, not only to survive but also to prosper in it. As a result, I forged a tough outer shell to conceal any sign of vulnerability, though the piercing looks and harsh words of others still left scars. I refused to give anyone the satisfaction of thinking they had gotten to me, that they had won or crushed my spirits. I am my own worst critic because of my propensity to project strength on the outside even when weakness lingers inside me. It's possible that what I truly needed from my father was a simple hug or other type of physical affection, so I wouldn't have to hide behind a hardened façade.

My dad could never see the world through my eyes, but it wasn't his job to do so. I feel his job was to be a shoulder to lean on, provide steadfast support, and deliver the tough love I needed to grow intellectually. My dad would often take me to a non-profit hospital about an hour and a half from where we lived to be fitted for my prosthetics. My dad would always fill the back seat of his beloved beige Cadillac with all my favorite stuffed animals. I kid you not, there would be ten to fifteen different stuffed animals, which he knew I needed for the long car ride. On the way, we would stop at McDonald's to get orange juice and a breakfast sandwich. It was our ritual. A ritual that he knew I loved.

When we were together, my father had a mystical way of calming my mind and making time stand still. He also had a habit of preaching the same things repeatedly:

"Why do you care what others think? Let them stare."

"Peanut, don't let them get to you."

"Peanut, don't forget how strong you are."

My father's rare indirect optimism and praise were never enough to compensate for the fact that I had to live with my imperfections.

I would hide my prosthetics even at the non-profit hospital. Isn't that crazy? I was finally surrounded by other imperfect kids like me, and I didn't even want them to judge me. I didn't want their parents to judge me . . . *the irony.*

At appointments, I would need to remove my prosthetics to try on new ones and walk around an open seating area to ensure everything fit properly. I would get a pit in my stomach while walking around with my prosthetics visible to everyone. It reminded me of school, where I was giving everyone something to stop and stare at.

Whenever I was being foolish, my dad would utter, "Kat, you are being ridiculous. Look around you, nobody cares."

I cared though! I let society define me and determine that I may never be accepted.

I'm the product of my own environment.

It never mattered how many trips we took a year to adjust my prosthetics—what mattered was getting the right fit. My dad was my fiercest advocate, constantly asking why I couldn't have access to the latest and greatest technology. In the patient room, he would sit in the chair reading and pointing to magazine articles, circling advanced prosthetic knees and say, "Peanut, you will have one of these someday."

I would sit there and offer a hopeful smile. In all honesty, my dad's dreams for me were bigger than mine. He believed I could walk better, live fuller, and move through life with confidence. However, I knew we didn't have access to that kind of innovation. I was simply thankful to have the essentials—prosthetics, that allowed me to live my life.

Unfortunately, the reality for many families is choosing between necessities such as food, rent, or transportation. In my case, it was the choice of affordability versus the advanced technology I needed. There are countless things people worry about, and I never want prosthetics to be one of them for me. *Money comes and goes, but my legs are not just tools—they are my lifeline.* That is why I remain humbly grateful with every step I take.

Throughout my childhood, my efforts were always directed toward gaining my father's approval and recognition and attaining his rare verbal affirmations. My desire was not to please myself or society, it was always and inevitably to please my dad. Even now, I constantly feel that there is a void that I am unable to fill. My emotions are my emotions. That's not self-doubt, that's pure honesty. My dad is *everything* to me.

My sisters never shared much interest in my dad's passions or hobbies, so I took it upon myself to step into this role. Whether it meant going to a bar to watch a game, cheering in a baseball venue, or learning how to swing a golf club, I was there. Because nothing compared to his love for golf, I always thought learning and playing the game—which he *still* loves unconditionally—would unlock the key to his heart. I continue to strive to receive physical affection and verbal affirmation from him to this day. However, it's possible that my dad doesn't have the capacity to give me the validations I seek because he doesn't receive the support or validation he desires from my sisters or mother. My family is its own collection of tangled knots.

I am beginning to come to terms with the fact that my father loved me without conditions in his own unique way. However, deep within, I have never felt genuinely loved before, whether it was from others or even from myself. I pour so much of myself into others, yet I've never had the wherewithal to pour into myself. I never had someone reciprocate the actions and emotions I put into them. It's been a lifelong journey for me to accept that, and I'm content with it because I know it won't change who I am. The power of love itself is hard to embrace or recognize when you haven't experienced it. I tend to give more than I get and I'm discovering that it's not the fault of anyone, just part of how things unfold sometimes.

I realize my dad has educated me in every aspect of my life. Therefore, as we both age, I am left questioning if I have learned enough from him or have the necessary tools to succeed without him. I notice I am not using his advice and teachings as much, but I know his lessons will serve me well in the future. I am now developing the ability to believe and understand that my existence is not solely for my father. I am on the right path heading in the right direction. I must have faith that he will always be with me, whether physically present or from heaven above. He will always be the one impetus who motivated me to thrive and not just survive. He will constantly remind me of my worth; he will continue to make me feel like Daddy's girl.

I was never raised to seek acceptance or affirmation, even though as a young imperfect girl, I yearned for them. Words, when chosen with care, carry the power to heal, to validate and anchor a soul seeking depth. I am coming to terms with the fact that my father's age may prevent me from ever hearing the affirmations I have hoped for. So, I am modifying my perspective. I am slowly finding peace in his presence rather than focusing on the words withheld. His love is demonstrated through consistent action and unwavering support. Although a part of me still aches for something he cannot or will not say, I am learning to understand the language of love that doesn't speak.

My heart is my own home-grown creation. No one gave it to me. Nothing is given. It is only earned. I strategically apply everything I acquire and learn to drive beneficial outcomes. I have chosen to be a light for others because of my father's lessons in giving and believing in myself. My dad's faith has taught me to trust in myself and in God's plan, knowing that God will wrap his arms around me when my father is no longer here to guide me.

Hang in there,
the imperfect you.
Remember, it's okay to
want to feel loved.
It's okay to give more
than you get. Just remember
to love yourself first.
Your purpose is to thrive
and not just survive.

Use the space below to let your thoughts flow freely.

Who is the constant in your life? The person who has always been there for you.

Name and describe the person:

____

____

____

____

____

How does your constant show their love or appreciation for you, and how do you reciprocate it?

Think about actions, words, or traditions you share:

____

____

How does this person influence how you give back and contribute to society?

Consider your daily life, work, community involvement, or personal mission:

THE LASTING IMPRESSION

There is always one teacher who leaves a lasting impression and is forever engraved in your memory. A teacher who had faith in you and saw something in you before you saw it in yourself. For me, that was my middle school gym teacher, Mr. Evans. He was known for his sharp sarcasm, quick wit, and genuine care for students.

My town has nine elementary schools, three middle schools, and one high school. Typically, students progress to the middle school aligned with their elementary school district. It is worth mentioning that in my case, both schools were within walking distance of my childhood home. However, instead of following the typical path, this special ed, imperfect girl was forced to pack her bags and travel across town. My town's illogical ideology uprooted my familiar surroundings, replacing them with distance and disconnect. I had difficulty fitting in at this school. My new placement in special ed felt more like a label rather than support, and it further isolated me. I was confronted with a new environment without any friends and having to rebuild from scratch. My new peers presented a sense of entitlement. They glided through the halls with confidence I could not fake. Teachers saw and praised them as I continuously faded into the background. I was invisible.

Most of the boys had inflated egos, and one moment still stings. One of the so-called popular boys pointed at me, laughing with his friends as I carefully sidestepped down the stairs. I guess I was some kind of joke to them. Gosh, why are young kids so cruel? Where do parents go wrong? Will the narrative and cycle ever change? Shouldn't society do better? These boys were in that transient phase of life where coolness felt like power, and they believed others around them would bend to their charm.

What is it about being different that always makes it so hard for others to accept?

Mr. Evans turned out to be my only salvation during this tumultuous time, though it took me a while to adjust to his tough love. He never sugarcoated anything. His honesty was hard to take at first, but it was exactly what I needed. Mr. Evans resembled my father in many ways. They both didn't want me to pay attention to other people's criticism and let it affect me. He pushed me to become the best version of myself. He knew I had the ability to achieve anything I set my mind to if I could just learn to ignore the negative external noise. Mr. Evans' humorous and sarcastic nature was infectious and had a long-term impact on me. I tend to be more reserved when meeting new people, but once I become comfortable, I develop a sarcastic and lighthearted demeanor, which I certainly learned from him.

It's unsurprising that I didn't have many friends in middle school. As I look back, I wonder if it was partially due to my inability to expect others to accept me when I didn't have the wherewithal to accept myself. My being enrolled in the special ed program didn't help either, because I was largely disconnected from the rest of the student population. All of my classes had the same group of students, including some with learning disabilities and others who also had behavioral issues. It seemed to be a catch-all group of misfits, as if the decision maker's thought process was, "Hey, this student is different, let's put them in special ed because they are not well-suited for traditional classes."

There were times when I felt a bit uneasy and had to remain extra vigilant of my surroundings. Thankfully, the skills and awareness I developed during my childhood being a keen observer helped me navigate certain situations. I'll never forget the moment when one of the boys, visibly agitated by something the teacher said, impulsively grabbed his pencil, walked toward me, and without warning stabbed me in my left arm with alarming aggression. Mind you, I am left-handed. I witnessed the situation unfolding and froze at my desk, making no sudden movement that might provoke him. Clearly, my decision failed, because I got caught in his crossfire. I cannot adequately describe the immediate trauma and excruciating pain I endured. A memory forever etched in my mind. Why was I the one he targeted? I guess I'll never know.

I was rushed to the nurse's office as tears began to gleam in my eyes, blood started to flow, and fear filled my veins. I remember worrying about whether I would die or experience any adverse effects from lead poisoning. I realize that sounds dramatic now, but I was a young teenager. I still have the everlasting scar on my left arm.

Mr. Evans made every effort to help me overcome my feelings of inferiority, loneliness, and defeat. He recognized my passion for sports and encouraged me to embrace my athleticism. Because others laughed at me, I felt discouraged and regularly wanted to quit gym activities. He would firmly but supportively tell me to get my head in the game. He motivated me to succeed and to never give up, despite others tormenting me and wanting me to fail. He offered me a daily sprinkle of no-nonsense wisdom and reminded me to never stop trying. He consistently preached "practice makes perfect."

Mr. Evans could always tell when I was not putting forth my best effort, and his humor had a mystical ability to make me smile and lift my spirits.

"Oh, I didn't know we were having a pity party today."

"Who gave you permission to be lazy today?"

"Kat, get your behind up! I don't care what so-and-so said."

"Take a lap. I don't care how long it takes because we both know you are more than capable of completing the activity."

Jeez! Looking back, he was a force of nature and ultimately right in his methods of empowering me.

There were occasions when I found it difficult to believe the things he said to me, but I knew it came from a place of care and that he didn't want me to internalize other's negative perceptions. When I had no one to sit with at lunchtime, he kindly let me sit in his office while he read his beloved newspaper, which he was rarely without. Even during gym class, he would walk around with it folded in his hands. I found it funny because he couldn't read it while shouting instructions during class, but perhaps it was not about reading at all, just emotional reassurance, like a security blanket.

I distinctly remember one time in gym class when he asked me to go to the library to pick up a copy of the newspaper, "Kat go down to the library and ask the librarian for a copy of the Herald and hurry back."

In this instance, I wasn't exactly the sharpest tool in the shed.

I made my way down to the library and told the librarian, "Mr. Evans would like me to pick up a copy of the heroin."

"A copy of what dear?" she said.

"The heroin," I reiterated.

"Okay, just wait right here."

She came back and said, "Okay, here is a copy of the *Herald.*" Apparently, she also called Mr. Evans about my unique request.

I ran back to class, and Mr. Evans stopped me in the hallway between his office and the gymnasium.

In a sarcastic tone and shaking his head he asked, "Kat are you trying to get me fired?"

"I got the paper like you wanted and did it as fast as I could," I replied while handing him the newspaper.

"Kat, what did you say to the librarian?"

"I told her you wanted a copy of the heroin."

Mr. Evans just sighed, rubbing his forehead. "It's called the HERALD."

I offered a quick smile and an apology as he stepped aside, pointing towards the gymnasium. As I walked toward the gym to re-join my class, my heart shattered because I looked at Mr. Evans as a father figure, and the thought of letting him down was devastating. (My guiding thought has always been to never disappoint anyone.) At that age, I didn't even know heroin was a drug. I must have missed that day in health class. When I eventually found out, I felt so stupid. Let's just say that was the first and last time I got the newspaper for him.

If it's not obvious, sports that involved the use of my upper body came easier than sports like soccer and track that relied on my lower body. I could throw a football, play basketball, and was good at wiffle ball and softball. Mr. Evans was the head coach of the football team—a role that came as no surprise after seeing his drill-sergeant style in gym class. He consistently encouraged me to stay involved in as many extracurricular activities as I could. Girls were given the opportunity to play on the football team in middle school. Now, before you jump to conclusions . . . no, I wasn't one of the girls who suited up to play. However, Mr. Evans did appoint me as team manager. I served as the coaches' right-hand person, supporting all aspects of team preparation and execution. During practices, I set up drills and transported equipment to and from the field. On game days, I assisted the quarterbacks on the sidelines by throwing the football to help them stay loose and ensured players stayed hydrated by providing water as needed. My role gave me a front-row seat to the action without bruises or bone-rattling tackles. I will admit I was grateful to avoid some hits the girls endured on the field.

As much as I enjoyed supporting the football team, I aspired to compete in my own way. After school, I sometimes found myself on the basketball court, sharpening my free throws, refining my dribbling skills, and simply losing myself in the rhythm of practice. My sister Samantha enjoyed playing basketball too. She would go to the park with me to play and assist me in improving my skills. As I grew up, Samantha made more of an effort to include me, but it often depended on whether she had other plans. Like many siblings, we had our fair share of arguments; it was just part of growing up together. Over time, something shifted with Samantha and she became more of my quiet protector. She wasn't always physically present, but when I confided in her, especially if someone wasn't treating me right, she never hesitated to stand up for me. She moved with a stronger sense of confidence and ensured we had time together.

Over time, Mr. Evans expressed to me that I was getting better and that my hard work was paying off. He was aware that I liked soccer, but he thought I should concentrate on a sport that was easier for me and one I felt confident in. He never told me to give up on soccer, just subtly steered me toward a sport I enjoyed that complimented my abilities.

Mr. Evans organized the annual three-on-three basketball fundraiser tournament, a big event that brought the school community together. He and the other gym teachers thought of me when they needed help with the fundraiser. Mr. Evans entrusted me to oversee the concession stand, a responsibility I did not take lightly. It meant a lot, especially considering I was in special ed. I remember asking Mr. Evans for a calculator, just in case someone had a substantial purchase. I was not proficient at calculating totals quickly in my head.

"A calculator? What do you need that for?" he sarcastically responded.

"I don't want to get in trouble by charging someone the wrong amount or giving back the wrong change," I said, giggling.

He went to his office and returned, tossing a calculator on the table with a smile. "You know how to use it, right?" His sarcasm at its best.

The tournament was for both boys and girls, and as you may have already guessed, I wanted to be a part of it. The only problem was I didn't have any girlfriends to team up with. One day during gym class, I was practicing my free throws alone when two tall, Black girls walked over and began talking to me. They asked me, an imperfect nobody, to join their team. Yes, *me*, Kat Floridia!

Let's pause for a moment to give some context. I am a white, handicapped female. It's important to remember that in this world, prejudice is felt by individuals who are different due to race, cognitive limitations, physical limitations, and many other reasons. At this juncture, it was shocking to be approached at all. It was even more shocking to be asked by two beautiful, tall, athletic Black girls. What led them to ask the only white, handicapped female to join their team?

Samantha was equally surprised and didn't believe me when I told her who had asked me to join their team. She giggled, covering her mouth with her right hand, and asked with teasing sarcasm: "Wait, they asked you? Are you sure?" Samantha, who is Black, was even more perplexed than me that I was chosen by these two girls out of all the students they could have asked. *So much for sisterly support!*

I remember standing there, frozen, gazing into the distance—eyes lingering on the distant corner of the gym, clutching the basketball in my hands.

The girls tried again. "Hey, did you hear us? Do you want to join our team? We need a point guard, and you can shoot."

My initial response was, "You're asking me?"

How did I know it wasn't a hoax? I was so used to being the butt of everyone's joke. I was accustomed to being invisible and being selected last because of my imperfections and inability to run fast. Did all of Mr. Evans' preaching about "practice makes perfect" finally pay off?

The girls laughed and said, "Yes, we are asking you. We want to win, and we always see you playing basketball. Come join our team, unless you already have one?"

I tried to remain calm, cool, and collected even though I was screaming joyfully inside. These girls had seen me practice. I wasn't invisible to them. Their athletic ability was always apparent to me because they were consistently chosen first on teams.

Still processing their question, I offered a hesitant nod and responded, "Okay, yeah sure, I will play on your team."

They replied, "Great, practice after school," and walked away as gym class was ending.

Puzzled by what transpired, I stopped by Mr. Evans's office on the way to my next class. I told him about the two girls who invited me to join their team.

With his trademark grin and touch of sarcasm, he asked, "Who's going to take care of the concession stand? I'm just joking. That's great." I asked him if he had any idea why they asked me or if he thought it was a ruse. He said, "Kat, I know those two young ladies, and they will probably be college athletes one day. They know talent when they see it. I told you practice makes perfect, and your skills have improved. Now get to your next class, I don't need your teacher blaming me for your tardiness."

The tournament kicked off the following week, and I was so nervous. I didn't want to disappoint the two girls who asked me, *yes me*, to play on their team. From the first game, our synergy was electric. We played with precision, heart, and grit. We advanced through the brackets one victory at a time. We dominated. All three of us were so driven to win, but for me, it was more than just winning. It was my opportunity to prove to all the other students that they should think twice before selecting me last again.

The thrill of sinking outside shots, driving to the basket, and lofting passes to my tallest teammate was unforgettable. Watching her dominate in the paint and rejecting every challenger was nothing short of amazing. The entire experience was exhilarating. Our relentless dedication and unwavering determination led us to the finals. The pressure was high as the spotlight fell on the final six girls battling it out on the main court. The game was a nail-biter from start to finish with both teams locked in. As the clock ticked down, I drove hard to the basket for a layup but rimmed out. My taller teammate grabbed the rebound and made a last-ditch effort to score, but it didn't fall.

We lost. It was heartbreaking. I blamed myself. *Did I overlook a teammate who might have been wide open?* Despite our disappointment, we hugged and marveled at how far we had made it together—a three-girl team, including me. Although our time together was short-lived, the memory remains a meaningful and positive experience in my life.

After the tournament ended, I gathered my belongings and stopped by Mr. Evans's office with my head hanging low. "We lost."

"I know," he said with a nod.

Mr. Evans stepped out from behind his desk, handed me a trophy and a brand-new Rawlings basketball, and shared a few sincere words. "I'm not giving you these out of sympathy, you earned them. The determination, heart, and confidence you showed on that court is why you earned this trophy even if the scoreboard didn't show it. You need to carry that confidence with you every day regardless of the obstacle. The Kat I watched out there didn't feel sorry for herself. She showed heart. You're a natural athlete. That's why those girls asked you to play on their team. Yes, you made it to the finals and lost, but you achieved so much more. You earned respect from everyone around you and stayed true to who you are. You exceeded your abilities. The Kat I saw out there is who I expect to see moving forward. Now go clean up the concession stand. I don't want you to think I am getting soft on you." Overwhelmed by joy, I wish I had leaped up and hugged Mr. Evans.

He exemplified the very essence of what it means to be a true coach. Though he pushed me relentlessly, I understood it was driven by genuine care for me. His tough love and sarcasm contributed to strengthening my self-esteem and made me realize my entire life was yet to be lived. He recognized a young girl who needed to boost her self-confidence and prevent others from diminishing her. He regularly told me what I needed to hear without sugarcoating anything. I began to comprehend his message that the road to greatness can be achieved in various ways. For me, Mr. Evans was the most sincere and genuine teacher, mentor, coach, and person I have ever met.

To this day, I still have the Rawlings basketball and trophy.

While writing this memoir, I discovered Mr. Evans had passed away unexpectedly. May he rest in peace and know that his humor and compassion will always stay with me. He has permanently secured a place in my heart.

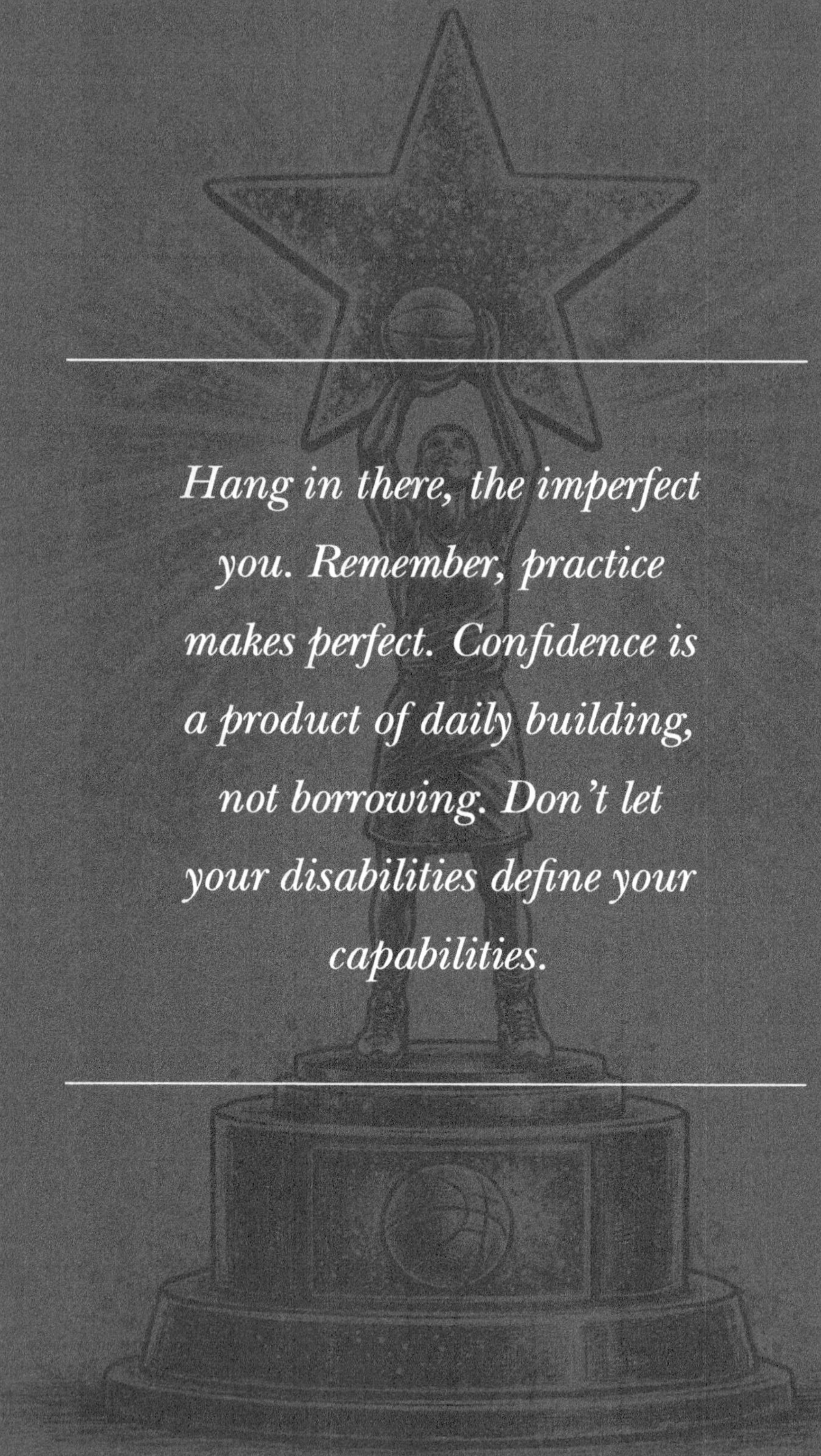

Hang in there, the imperfect you. Remember, practice makes perfect. Confidence is a product of daily building, not borrowing. Don't let your disabilities define your capabilities.

Use the space below to let your thoughts flow freely.

Did you have a teacher that genuinely believed in you?

Describe their lasting impression on you.

As part of society, how can you personally contribute to changing the negative narrative?

If you saw someone imperfect, how would you address it with your children, spouse, or peers?

What parts of yourself do you hide from others? Why?

What would it take for you to have the confidence to share them?

Is there a sport or activity (drama club, basketball, art club, chorus, etc.) you wanted to be part of?

What made you hesitate? What held you back from participating?

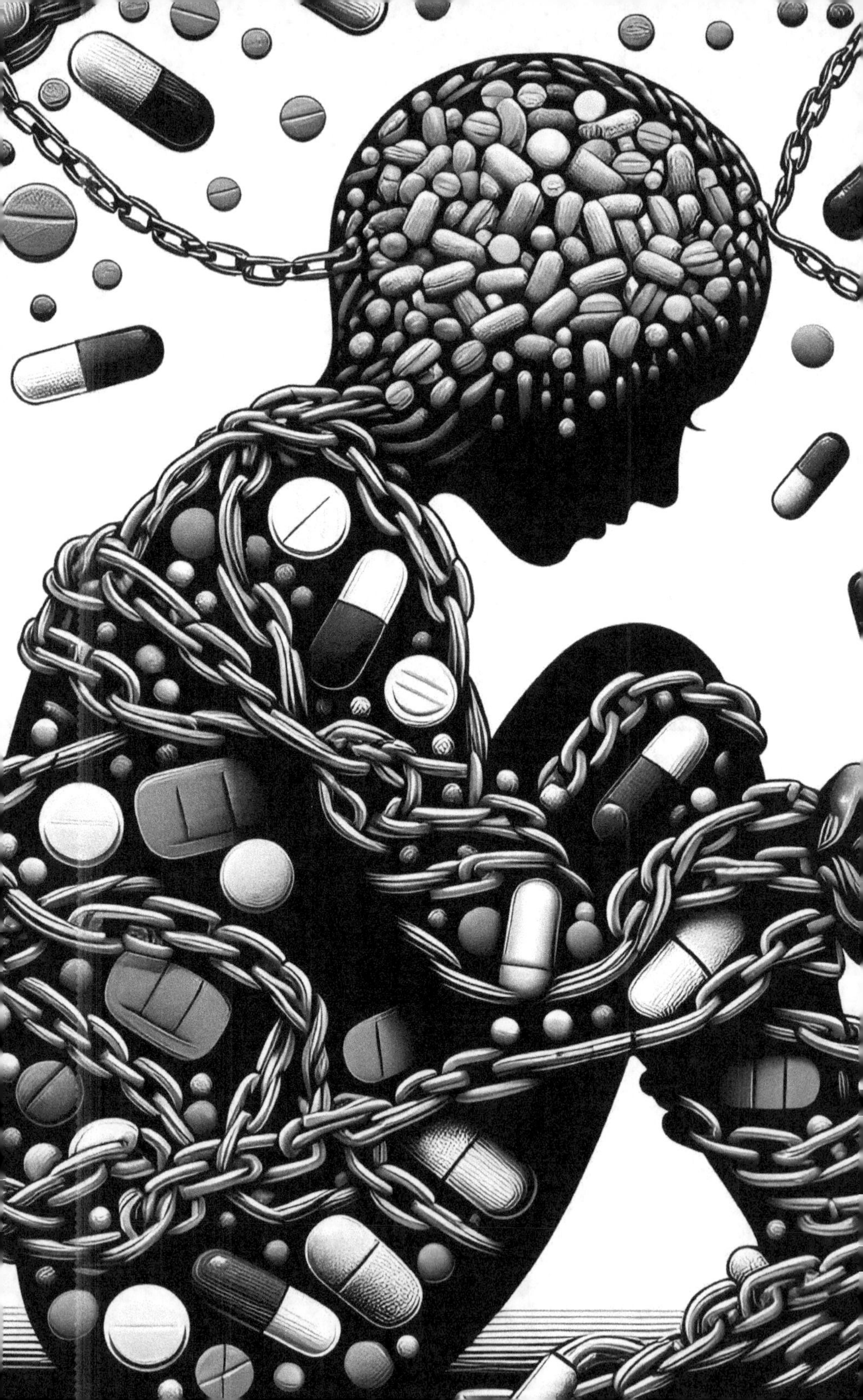

THE DARKEST HOURS

During my earliest years, until about age eight, my father and sisters shielded me from the reality of my mother's mental health struggles. But when I was nine, I felt as though a negative switch flipped inside her. That year, 2001, the sudden death of my cousin triggered a sharp and devastating decline in my mother's mental state. At the time, I couldn't fully understand the extent of her transformation, but the signs were unmistakable. Her behavior became more erratic and distant. She withdrew from me, lost focus, and seemed more emotionally disconnected from all of us. I could also sense that her profound deterioration drove my father and sisters further away.

Over the years, my mother grappled with the challenges of motherhood, and our family learned to navigate the ebb and flow of her good and bad days for what they were worth. She battles depression and has long struggled with addictive tendencies. At various points, she developed dependencies on extreme weight loss (anorexia), compulsive long-distance walking, alcohol, and prescription medication. While writing my memoir, I discovered my mother had a difficult childhood due to the loss of her parents. Her mother passed away at just twenty-seven years old, and her father was killed at forty. These devastating losses struck my mother when she was only seven and eighteen, respectively. Her father's physical abuse and mother's neglect also left deep emotional scars, making it nearly impossible for her to heal from the traumas of her childhood. As a result, she never developed emotional resilience or the understanding of compassion needed to be a nurturing mother.

My family became fed up with her illness and insufficiencies. One by one, they distanced themselves, leaving me as the last person who somewhat believed in her ability to persevere and overcome her demons. Between the ages of fifteen and eighteen, I was thrust into adulthood.

While most of my peers navigated high school with typical teenage concerns, I was learning how to care for my mother because no one else would. She had been abandoned by everyone except me. At the end of the day, I held onto my truth that she was my mother; that was enough for me.

The next four years played out like an unsettling movie in my household—dark, disjointed, and painful. Have you ever witnessed a relative seep into their lowest despair, to the point where they're almost nonexistent? Have you ever stared into the face of someone barely clinging to life? Close your eyes. Picture yourself at a funeral, standing over a casket. The room is hushed. Your loved one lies cold and pale. Now open your eyes. You're not at a funeral, you're in your mother's bedroom. And she's not gone . . . yet . . . but she's always on the verge. Her body is frail, her breath shallow, her presence flickering like a candle in the wind. And this isn't a moment. This is your everyday. Years of waking up to grief that haven't finished arriving. Years of mourning someone who's still alive. Years of speculating whether your mother would live to see another day. Years of speculating whether *you* would survive.

It's important to remember that my mother rescued the imperfect me when I was eighteen months old. Now it was my turn to repay the favor and help rescue her. My mother was instrumental in keeping my light bright at a young age, and now it was up to me to ensure her light was restored. This quest was not an easy one. I had to create a path for my mother to strive to be one percent better each day and to recognize that steadfast commitment could lead to remarkable achievement.

In high school, I started to rebel a bit. What teenager doesn't? I grew tired of being in special education classes. The environment was nothing like the classrooms I had experienced in elementary or middle school. Instead of learning, we spent our time playing games with no real educational purpose. It was a joke. I couldn't comprehend why I had to endure bullying from peers outside the program while feeling I didn't fit within it. After countless tears and heartfelt pleas, my parents finally arranged a meeting with the vice principal and the special education staff. My parents advocated for me to be removed from the program. The meeting was tense, but in the end I was unenrolled and allowed to attend traditional classes with the rest of the student body. As my story continues, I'll leave it up to you as the reader to determine if this was the most sensible decision for my grades and ultimately my future. Adapting to regular classes proved far more difficult than I had anticipated. I couldn't fully invest in my education while burdened by the weight of hidden turmoil at home. Each day, I would leave school only to return to the haunting sight of my mother's seemingly lifeless body.

The world has a cruel way of reminding us that trauma doesn't simply fade; it lingers and is etched into our senses. A familiar sound or scent can awaken memories we thought were once buried. For me, the smell of Greek yogurt or a loud thud triggers memories of my mother's darkest hours. During my mother's stupors, Greek yogurt was her go-to meal for breakfast, lunch, and dinner. She ate it like a kid, licking the lid and her fingers while taking large, messy spoonfuls that occasionally spilled onto her, the bed, and the floor. The mess was a result of her being high on whatever pills she was taking that day. For weeks, the smell of Greek yogurt lingered throughout the house, making me gag. To this day, the mere scent of Greek yogurt turns my stomach, and I still find it difficult to eat.

As for the loud thud, imagine your mother barely being able to stand on her own two feet and diving head-first into a wall, causing blood to drip down from her forehead.

CRASH, BOOM, BANG!

The young, imperfect me would stand in the hallway and ask, "Mom, are you okay?"

"I'm fine. I just tripped," my mother would mutter.

My father would shake his head in frustration and sarcastically say, "Yeah, sure, you just tripped."

My mother would search for anything to grab hold of to try and maintain her equilibrium. She would shuffle her feet, swaying back and forth, because she would be so far gone in her stupor that she had no stability. There were even times she crawled on the floor like a toddler with glassy eyes and unkempt hair to get around in the dark. In the dead of night, I would keep my bedroom door cracked open to make sure she was okay.

THUD! THUD! THUD!

My mother, in a state of impairment, had a tendency to fall in the bathroom when attempting to stand and maintain her balance. The noise was deafening. I could hear her toiletries fall to the floor as she scrambled to regain her composure, reaching for anything in arm's length. Moments later, I would hear my father's heavy footsteps echo down the hallway, each step pulsing with irritation. I knew what was next—his sharp, raised voice yelling at her, not out of concern, but out of anger. I will be the first to admit he failed when it came to caring for my mother. He was checked out at that point in their marriage. My dad only had so much patience and had grown tired from the countless years of my mother's drama and turbulent tendencies. I believe there are many of us who lack the skills, education, and knowledge required to recognize and comprehend someone's mental health illness.

He coped with her by lashing out verbally, and I can't say I blame him—she can be quite difficult to deal with. When frustrated, he would raise his voice and hurl insults at her. "Look at yourself. Do you think Kat wants to see you like this? Pathetic," he would say. Then he would bend down behind my mother, slide his arms under her armpits, and lift her with care back to bed. They would often exchange curse words because my mother would mumble something under her breath, and my father, already on edge, would snap at the slightest provocation.

"Stop taking your bleeping pills! You need help! We cannot live like this!" he would screech.

"Just go! You don't care about me. I don't want to be here anyway," my mother would reply in tears.

Each night a piece of my soul died. I would close my door slowly and lay awake in my bed. My father would slam my mother's bedroom door so hard it would shake the house.

Let's pause. I don't want to give you the wrong impression of my dad. He is a good man. I have a strong and loving relationship with him. His relationship with my mother was complex, and his reactions to her behavior were rooted in long-standing frustration.

Over the years, my parents became more distant, and my father slept on the couch. They were supposed to get a divorce, but the legal paperwork was never signed or processed. My father could never really divorce my mother anyway, because he is a religious man who believes a marriage is a union for life—for better for worse.

Samantha was sixteen and I was thirteen when our parents sold our childhood home. This was my mother's undertaking. She then asked my father to move out, and he moved in with relatives. He couldn't afford child support, so my mother received all the money from the sale of the house and assumed responsibility for raising us. The money was quickly drained from mom's bank account by purchases of mysterious pills and shopping at QVC. Her erratic habits continued. Samantha was fortunate to have friends who saved her from our mother's unstable conduct by giving her somewhere to escape. I, on the other hand, remained tethered to the house, burdened with the unspoken duty of tending to our mother's well-being.

Though I was the only person who offered my mother unwavering care and support, I was never her favorite. She always leaned toward Samantha and my oldest sister. And while it may be common belief that parents do not have a favorite child, actions speak louder than words. Samantha had a plethora of advantages, including a bigger bedroom, flat-screen TV, the newest cell phone, special treatment, and anything she wanted. My mother attempted to buy Samantha's love, hoping she would become an ally. Unfortunately for both of us, she never realized she already had one in me.

Samantha possessed the ability to manipulate my mother to obtain what she desired before escaping to freedom. When Samantha wasn't around, my mother would make an effort to contact my oldest sister in hopes of rebuilding their relationship. I felt defeated. I often bottled up my emotions, causing me to hide and cry in pain. I was the sole person who showed both concern for and faith in her. I was the only one who stood by her, though she never realized it. I questioned if there was something amiss with me and why I wasn't enough.

It's normal for us to experience moments of despair. It's alright to feel fractured. I've learned it's acceptable to not be okay all the time. It's acceptable to be vulnerable. It's acceptable to express your emotions and cry your heart out. My life story is my story. Each of us has a unique story with its own battle scars. However, it's up to us to not let our trauma define us.

* * *

In high school, the athletic department became my sanctuary, a place where I could belong despite my disability and inability to make a team. Thanks to the athletic director, I was introduced to several coaches who oversaw the women's basketball, soccer, softball, and lacrosse teams. They welcomed me to their programs and appointed me as team manager, entrusting me with responsibilities such as maintaining stat logbooks for individual players during games and assisting with drills during practice. Although the players were always kind and respectful, I wasn't one of them, and that divide shaped the nature of our interactions. However, I developed strong relationships with the coaches and athletic trainers, who treated me as a vital part of their team. They held me to the same standards as the players, expecting me to show up for practice and board the bus on time for away games. It gave me a sense of purpose. I felt I was contributing to something that mattered and was bigger than myself.

One of the biggest obstacles I faced was allowing athletics to take precedence over my education. As a result, my academic performance suffered. Looking back, I realize that sports offered me a rare sense of freedom—an escape from the difficulties I was experiencing at home. It became an outlet, my refuge, even if it came at the cost of not achieving good grades. My thought process was if I wasn't excelling in academics or making a significant difference at home, why should I not be entitled to participate in something that I thoroughly enjoyed—like the athletic teams.

I was never taught how to study or given the support I needed if I struggled. Instead of offering guidance, some teachers would simply give me a D-plus and wash their hands of me. There was no further mentoring from them. In traditional classes, I noticed there were very few teachers who were willing to go that extra mile. Rather than offering support, they chose to share gossip about their students openly among their colleagues. It's hard to differentiate who was worse, the so-called adults or the mean, tight-knit student cliques.

I'll never forget the day I walked into math class wearing long capris, only for my teacher to notice my prosthetics. She murmured something under her breath, then drifted to the corner, arms crossed, leaning against the wall as she whispered loudly to the teacher's aide about seeing my prosthesis for the first time. The look they shared said more than words ever could. I sat quietly with my head down, pretending to work on the class assignment, attempting to suppress tears as best as I could. Their behavior, on the one day I had a smidge of confidence to try on capris, left me degraded. It was yet another brutal reminder of the world's cruelty and how difficult it is to feel comfortable in my own skin. It rekindled memories of my youth in the park where mothers first noticed my prosthetics and doubted my abilities. It deepened my despair that the world would never accept me. *Could I ever get a break? Could somebody love me for me? Could somebody accept me as I am, regardless of my flaws?*

My hardships and inner turmoil were beyond anyone's understanding. The slightest stare or comment would have a profound effect on me. As I grew up, I mastered the art of suffering in silence, learning to carry pain inward and keep it hidden. Over time, criticizing myself turned into a habit. It became impossible to silence the harsh, negative voices in my head.

Our own self-criticism is a product of our surroundings.

No one knew of the personal surges and retreats I experienced daily, nor did they care to inquire about or monitor my well-being. The questions, "How are you

Kat? Seriously, how are you?" were never really meant for me. Neither was the offering of a simple hug. The smallest gesture or acknowledgement could have conveyed they saw me and were here for me. Instead, I carried the weight of resilience alone, tasked with staying strong not just for myself, but also for my mother. Unaware of the depth of their abandonment, my father and sisters left my mother behind—and in doing so, left me too. Being responsible for my mother was a burden. I had everything to lose, and the only thing I clung to was a fragile hope for my mother's recovery. I felt like a small sloth hanging from a tree, slowly moving, trying to climb and survive.

We were impoverished, even though my dad will never admit it.

We had a childhood home; my mom chose to sell it and blow through the money.

We lived in subsidized housing after getting evicted from multiple apartments.

We had state health insurance.

We qualified for food stamps, but my father was too proud to use them. He found it embarrassing. He preferred to ask friends or family for assistance.

We barely had enough to eat in the house. I would rummage for a few crumpled dollars to buy a snack at school.

For four long and arduous years, I endured the circumstances forced upon me. The burden I carried was immense. Trapped in the immediacy of each moment, I found myself unable to envision what the future might hold. A typical day for me looked like: wake up tired, skip breakfast, search for a few bucks hoping I could eat, put a brave face on, find a way to school, pretend to concentrate in class, attend a team activity, and eventually return home to check on my mother and tidy up the house. It was exhausting, but it had to be done.

I wrestled with my own imperfections, burying my emotions to stay strong for my mother. I never knew what version of her I would find when I walked through the door. Most days, I was confronted with her limp body surrounded by pill bottles scattered everywhere. Opening her bedroom door was daunting, as the air was thick with the sharp, sour stench of Greek yogurt, body odor, and God knows what else. A palpitation would grip my chest, and my thoughts would race. I would yell, "Mom, Mom, Mom!" until she muttered something and I knew she was still alive. She hated water and refused to stay hydrated, leaving her mouth parched and her lips split and peeling. As a result of being under the influence and lacking self-care, her appearance was that of a disheveled, fictional, crazed wild-looking scientist wearing pink pajamas.

I still carry a vivid recollection of finding my mother unresponsive throughout my teenage years—her face bruised and discolored, her body curled on her side, her left arm dangling over the edge of the bed. Pill bottles scattered across the floor in silent witness. A single thought pierced through my mind: *This is it. This is the end.* Tears blurred my vision as panic surged and I fumbled to call my dad. Had she finally pushed herself past the brink of no return? I collapsed into a chair in the living room, consumed by grief, unable to do anything but cry while waiting for my father to arrive. On his way, he dialed 911, and by the time he arrived, the ambulance was already there. I watched as the emergency personnel rushed into her room, their voices sharp and urgent, calling her name again and again, desperate to pull her back. Then came the moment I'll never forget, the paramedics wheeling her past me on the gurney, her body motionless but with shallow breathing. Helplessness washed over me, leaving me numb. It felt as though the world had stopped moving, except for them carrying her away. As I reflect, I ask myself "Why didn't I do more?

Why wasn't I smarter? Why did I just sit there weak and in tears?" Maybe it didn't matter. Maybe there was nothing more I could have done.

My mom survived that crisis, but the hospital required her to enter rehabilitation. She spent many years moving in and out of different facilities. My dad and I were the only ones who visited her. Each rehab center presented its own challenges, and visiting was often difficult for me because the facilities housed a wide range of patients. Many were dealing not only with substance abuse, but also with other serious mental health disorders, which made the environment unpredictable and overwhelming. But I stayed strong and kept visiting her.

Unfortunately, the vicious cycle never stopped. The ambulance became a familiar presence, almost as if it were on speed dial.

She would overdose on pills.

She would undergo another psychological evaluation in the emergency room—an experience she despised, convinced the physician who saw her time and again had something against her.

She would be transferred to a rehab facility.

She would be discharged, come home, only to relapse once more.

I was the parent. I never truly had a mother. I had a patient. At times, it felt as though I completed a residency, caring for her day after day. Perhaps I could have pursued a career in medicine, because I had lived it.

Over the years, I tried to reshape how others saw my mother, hoping to soften their judgment of her even as I struggled with how society perceived me. I can't say I succeeded, but I knew I didn't want my mother to be defined by her illness or condemned by others. My hope was that she would just get better.

Despite my efforts to care for my mother, she often directed her frustration toward me when her mood darkened or she sank deeper into her stupor. My mom once yelled at me from across the other side of the house, "I wish you'd get hit by a car and die." (A memory forever etched in my mind.)

You would think that would have been my final straw.

However, it's not easy to give up on someone who finds comfort in their own brokenness. No matter how she treated me, I couldn't resist the urge to care for and protect her. For God's sake, she is my *mother*.

During her worst overdoses, she lashed out not only at me but also at the medical staff—a behavior that never worked in her favor. She would end up restrained, with an officer stationed outside her door, something I later understood was part of being placed on suicide watch. After she sobered up, I would visit and ask the staff to release her from her restraints. They refused. I would ask them to turn on the television for her, but instead they entered her room to remove the phone and strip away any wires. I remember voicing my outrage, convinced they were being unreasonable. At the time, I was still so naive, unable to fully grasp the gravity of the situation. I felt obligated to defend my mother because no one else would.

It is in my nature to defend those I care for, even when I forget to guard myself. At the same time, I recognized that my struggle was not only for protection, but for her love and acceptance.

In the midst of another overdose, I remember calling 911 and telling the dispatcher I thought my mother had *accidentally* taken too many pills; I couldn't fathom telling the dispatcher she had intentionally overmedicated herself. I sat beside my mother on the bed, cradling her as she trembled, disoriented and unaware of where she was. I tried to reassure her, whispering there was nothing to worry about, I had told the dispatcher it was an accident and that she had simply taken too many pills. My father stood in the doorway, shaking his head in frustration, and said, "Kat, they're never going to believe that. Look at her. Pathetic."

He asked my mother how many more times she planned to put the family through this cycle. I ignored him. To me, it seemed cruel to keep striking at someone who was already broken, fragile, and down. My mother remained at the center of everything, even as her awareness faded and her eyes grew vacant. Her personality, addiction, and illnesses invoked the attention she seemed to crave.

It's ironic that while my mother was on suicide watch at the hospital, no one was aware I had suicidal thoughts. What was the purpose of my presence and what did my future hold? How was I supposed to prosper? Why would I ask for help for me? My miserable existence, eroded by constant stares, pointing fingers, and cruel, debilitating comments, stripped away my sense of identity. No one truly understood the weight my mother's many disorders placed on my mind, my grades, and the entire course of my high school years.

Is there a genuine person in your life who you can trust in times of need? Is there someone who you know without a doubt will be there for you? If there is, cherish them because not everyone is fortunate enough to have someone they can depend on. I am dependent on me, myself and I. I'll continue to show up for those who need me with the belief the favor will never be reciprocated. I've come to terms with it and am content with it. Sometimes it's easier to opt for peace. We may not all find that one person, but we can still be that one person for others.

* * *

At the start of my junior year, I began thinking about a four-year college. To my dismay, my guidance counselor implied I was only worthy of community college, which is fine for some, but I had higher aspirations. Her negative comments became the driving force behind my determination to improve my grades. She never believed in my potential. It's paradoxical that for someone who worked in education and was responsible for *guiding* students, she wasn't very proficient at it. She was no different than the countless others who doubted and underestimated me. With a single glance at my falling grades, she decided she had me all figured out. To me, it felt as though she should be fired for her lack of support, simply because I wasn't one of her prized AP students. *Really? How dare she!* This woman got under my skin. Regardless of a student's academic record, counselors should actively engage in their education by offering encouragement, providing assistance, connecting them with resources, and instilling hope. After all, the true purpose of working in education is to nurture and empower the future leaders of tomorrow. Isn't that what it's all about?

My guidance counselor dismissed me as insignificant, urging me to do only the bare minimum to make it to graduation. To judge superficially is to invite unfairness and to overlook the genuine value within a person. I did not take this moment lightly. It ignited my mental resilience. Whenever I found myself on the verge of defeat, I drew strength from God, who empowered me to fight back. My objectives became clear: to attend a four-year college and prove to my guidance counselor, and to anyone else who doubted my individual worth, that no one should judge another or underestimate their will. I had to find my own pendulum balance.

While writing my memoir, my mother expressed she could have done better. My response was simple, yet profound: She couldn't have done better. One individual's illness is something that belongs to all of us.

Hang in there, the imperfect you. You never know when your unwavering dedication and selflessness will be the guiding light for someone in need. Always remember forgiveness is a gift you give yourself.

Use the space below to let your thoughts flow freely.

Have you prioritized someone else's needs over your own?

Was it a positive or negative experience? Did you lose part of yourself in the process?

Can you recall a time when proving naysayers wrong became a source of motivation?

Did you feel confident in yourself? Were you proud of yourself for standing strong?

Have you ever felt abandoned?

Where did it happen (work, school, home, etc.)? Describe your feelings. Explain your journey through it.

BURDEN OF MY BODY

This chapter is dedicated to all the imperfect souls who have spent countless hours watching *Law & Order SVU*, never believing they might one day find themselves in a role of the victim—and wishing, if that moment unfortunately ever came, that a fictional character like Captain Benson would step in to empower them and fight for justice.

Justice was not served for me, and this remains my deepest wound. A scar etched not just in memory, but in my identity. It stands as a silent testament that trauma and transformation can coexist. To anyone who doubts the reality of post-traumatic stress disorder (PTSD), let me assure you, it is heartbreakingly real. It isn't just anxiety or fear. It is a constant, involuntary state of hyper-awareness, where my mind is locked in fight or flight. Why? Because the vivid flashbacks of my uninvited and unrelenting sexual assault have not faded. PTSD is not a weakness. It's a wound. And like any wound, it deserves to be seen, understood, and treated with compassion.

* * *

I remember feeling a mix of excitement and anxiety as I prepared to attend college. I always thought it was a far-fetched dream for someone like me. I had graduated high school with a 1.8 GPA because my priority was caring for my mother. The college application process required two essays and one simple dream. All I hoped for was that one college, just one, would be empathetic and give this disabled, reserved girl, crippled with anxiety, a chance to see her potential. I applied to twelve colleges and was accepted into three to four small private schools. Although I had no idea how I would afford it, I refused to let that uncertainty discourage me. I chose to attend a small private business school in the middle of nowhere. The school population was predominantly men, but that didn't matter to me. I had two goals: to make my dad and

Samantha proud, and to prove my high school guidance counselor wrong.

I was fortunate to receive a scholarship and financial aid, along with a small private loan generously co-signed by my supportive aunt and uncle. These resources enabled me to embark on a new chapter of life filled with hope, opportunity, and a renewed sense of freedom. In one of my college essays, I expressed my deep passion for sports, which led my admissions counselor to connect me with the athletic department. Additionally, my financial aid package included federal work study, offering me the chance to earn income through an on-campus job, an invaluable opportunity for low-income students, like me, to help cover some college expenses.

I secured a job in the athletic department's equipment room, which allowed me to move in early and become immersed in campus life before classes even began. The position was perfect, and I always looked forward to my shifts because it gave me the chance to interact with the athletes of both genders. One of the highlights of my position was standing on the sidelines during the football games, soaking in the roar of the crowd, the sharp play calls, and the crisp Friday night air under the stadium lights. What I hadn't realized was that beneath its seemingly vibrant and welcoming surface, this environment also provided the perfect conditions for players like Scotty to prey upon and exploit women.

At work, I got to know most of the athletes and the equipment they relied on. As time went on, the players grew more familiar with me, and our interactions became more relaxed and fun. We would joke around, share some laughs, and built a sense of camaraderie. The football players were the goofiest, and I soon found myself memorizing their equipment and jersey numbers. Players whose information I hadn't memorized yet would say, "Kat, you don't remember mine, but you remember his?" It was all in good fun.

Scotty and a few others regularly tried to charm me and the other two girls with their smooth talk and playful flirting, but we would simply laugh. As a woman in college, who wouldn't be interested in being flirted with?

However, there is a clear line between playful flirting and behavior that crosses into pressure or force.

On campus, there was a designated residents hall for freshmen. My room was tucked in the corner of the third floor near the stairs, and it couldn't have been better. I had a double room all to myself. Although I initially expected it to be lonely, I quickly came to appreciate a space to feel safe in my solitude. Having my own space meant no distractions, no awkward small talk, and the comfort of knowing I could unwind in peace and move freely with or without my prosthetics.

Scotty lived in the same residence hall, so we bumped into each other all the time. Our encounters were reliably filled with sarcastic banter and laughter with witty jabs. He was cute, which made our interactions feel like harmless, playful flirting. We had a tendency of crossing paths in one of the many laundry rooms scattered throughout the building. Watching guys like Scotty struggle through the basics of laundry was amusing to me. I would end up giving an impromptu tutorial on separating darks from lights and the art of folding. Those moments turned routine chores into unexpectedly funny and entertaining exchanges.

One afternoon, Scotty knocked on my door to ask me for a favor. He said he needed my help doing his laundry, just transferring clothes from the washer to the dryer and folding them. He said he either had an away game or practice—this is one detail I don't remember—and he wasn't coming back until later. I didn't give it much thought at the time; we were friendly enough, and I was already accustomed to doing laundry for the players in the equipment room.

I laughed softly and said, "Sure, no problem, but you'll owe me."

"Great, thank you so much," he replied.

Later that evening, Scotty returned. I dropped off his laundry, and he thanked me for my help. I had just finally started to settle in for the night when I heard a knock at my door, sometime between nine thirty and ten. I opened the door to find Scotty standing there. I was surprised to see him.

"Hey, what's up?" I asked.

"Not much. I wanted to see what you were up to."

"I'm just finishing up some homework and was going watch a TV show or play a video game."

"Cool, well, you wanna hang out? You did help me with my laundry."

"Sure, but I'm not staying up that much longer."

He strolled in without hesitation and flopped onto my bed, even though this was our first time hanging out together. I grabbed the remote and leaned back against my desk, arms crossed, watching him settle in like this was just another ordinary night in his own room.

"What do you want to watch?" I asked.

"It doesn't matter to me. Hey, you know, you can sit over here with me," he said, patting the bed.

I remember smirking, a hint of sarcasm in my voice as I shot back, "Yeah, I know. It's my room." I walked over slowly, handing him the remote as I eased onto the edge of my bed, wary and deliberate. Before I could even get comfortable, Scotty sprawled out like he owned the place. I gave him a snide look and said, "Wow, just make yourself at home, why don't you?"

This part is where my memory is kind of fuzzy. While he was sprawling out and without warning, he pulled me close, wrapping his arm tightly around my right side. The next thing I knew, I was lying next to him and he was forcing his tongue into my mouth. I tried to push him away, but somehow, he got on top of me. As I stared at the white concrete ceiling, fluorescent lights shining in my eyes, a wave of fear surged through me, paralyzing every muscle. Scotty suddenly sprang off the bed and quickly pulled the curtains shut. Then, without hesitation, he climbed back on top of me, yanking off my shirt and bra as his aggression escalated. I was in the fight of my life. I kept repeating "Stop!" and pushing against him with everything I had, but I was powerless. I felt both physically and emotionally numb. My mind and soul left my body, and I blacked out.

When he attempted to pull down my pants, I began to come to. I somehow found the will and the strength to hold up the waistband of my gray sweatpants. Thank God for me!

He unbuttoned his jeans and let them fall. I clenched my eyes shut, pressing my lips together, gripping the waistband of my gray sweatpants with every ounce of strength I had. Then with unsettling confidence, he said, "I have to finish," and leaned in, trying to kiss me. I turned my head and silently prayed this was all a nightmare. He grabbed both my breasts and slid his erection in between them. He started moaning and ejaculated all over my chest.

When fear courses through your veins, every second stretches, turning minutes into hours. Those thirty to forty-five minutes felt like an eternity. I felt like I lost the battle. Once he finally finished, he nonchalantly got up and got dressed like it was nothing—*like I was nothing.*

I laid there half-naked, paralyzed, numb, and scared. As soon as I heard my door slam shut, I stood up, locked it, and placed my desk chair in front of it. I removed my prosthetics and immediately went into the shower. Curled in a fetal position, I let my pool of tears and the shower water blend together until the scalding hot water turned my skin red, hoping the burn on the outside would match the ache within. I put a whole bar of Ivory soap in my mouth to wash out the filth. I intensely and repeatedly scrubbed my body until the water turned cold, trying to remove a layer of skin off my tainted and abused body. *How dare he!*

I turned off the water and crawled onto the cold, tile bathroom floor, letting the chill seep into my skin as I just lay there . . .

Naked.

Defeated.

Paralyzed.

Helpless.

Ashamed.

Exhausted by tears and pain, I drifted into sleep. Around 2:00 a.m., I awoke, still aching. I put on my pajamas, stripped the sheets from my bed and set an alarm for my 8:00 a.m. class. In the morning, I looked like hell. But I reminded myself of my goals: to make my father proud and earn a successful education. The imperfect me had no choice but to move on, suffer silently, and attend class.

I knew if I said anything it would turn into one of those "she said, he said" situations, and I asked myself, "Do I really want to be *that* girl?" That handicapped, imperfect girl who accuses a football player of sexual assault? Given the size of the school, reporting it would have made me tomorrow's headline. I wasn't ready to give people another reason to scrutinize me.

A week passed. Scotty had the audacity to show up at my door, like I forgot about what happened. And me? I was still naive enough to answer. But this time, I cracked it open only enough to see his face and let him know I was still standing.

"What do you want?"

He leaned against the blue doorframe with the same cocky smirk, like he hadn't shattered anything. "Got any salt for my takeout?"

I rolled my eyes. "No," I said flatly, and before he could say another word, I shut the door and locked it. I thought to myself, *This boy is so brazen . . . like what . . . what the HELL?* In this pivotal moment, it became painfully evident that Scotty truly believed he'd done nothing wrong.

I was dumbfounded.

I was speechless.

I was appalled.

I was forever scarred.

I had endured an immense amount of agony throughout my life—cruel comments and the haunting image of my mother's seemingly lifeless body—but this pain was different. It wasn't just emotional or circumstantial, it was visceral. A raw, unrelenting ache that defied understanding. It consumed me, left me disoriented, as if my mind were unraveling thread by thread. I wanted to reach out, to ask for help, but I didn't know how.

So . . . what did I do to bury my pain? Well, I was in college, and the best way to fit in was to drink alcohol. Boy, did I hate the taste of alcohol.

I still remember my very first drink being a warm Jack Daniel's. I had never experienced heartburn until Mr. Jack Daniel was introduced into my life. To fit in with the cool kids, I had to either put up or shut up, and that's exactly what I did. I would tag along to parties with girls who were acquaintances more than friends. I sensed I was the ugly friend they brought along because they felt bad for me. I'd fade into the background, unnoticed and unimportant, like the girl at a school dance who sits alone at the table, pretending not to care that no one asked her to dance. I accepted that this was my place. In all honestly, I don't think I ever wanted another boy to look at me again. I went to the parties not for the company, but for the free booze, hoping the alcohol would dull the ache and blur the memories of that awful night. To get drinks down, I used chasers to mask the burn. At one party, a girl showed me how to mix drinks that dulled the strong alcohol taste, but I could still taste it. The mornings after were brutal, plagued by wicked hangovers that left me hollow. But drinking was my only path to tranquility.

I lived a double life, and to this day, I struggle to explain how I managed it. During the day, I was a model student, attending lectures, finishing assignments and clocking in at work. I wore the uniform of a quiet, studious college student, blending in with ease. But when night fell, especially Thursdays through Sundays, I became a lost binge drinker. The feeling of being inebriated stimulated me, leading to my fair share of blackouts. I thought I was someone else. I enjoyed being someone else. That someone else felt free of her existence. There were nights when the alcohol didn't just numb me, it ignited some anger. I remember punching my fist into the cement wall in my dorm, the impact fracturing two knuckles on my right hand. I still have flat knuckles that serve as a reminder. In moments of desperation, I also resorted to self-inflicted pain, once banging my head against the wooden bathroom door until a black eye bloomed across my face. I knew I was spiraling. The façade I wore was slipping, and I couldn't tell how much longer I could maintain my dual lifestyle.

It ultimately was a mixture of red wine and Sprite that broke me. I couldn't keep what happened to me a secret any longer. The mental anguish was torture. During their nightly rounds, two female resident assistants stumbled upon me in a stairwell, soaked in tears, drunk on red wine. Despite not knowing these girls, I felt a sense of comfort the moment one of them sat beside me. Her soft voice and caring demeanor made it easy for me to confide in her. I can't recall if I told her Scotty's name, but I do remember explaining what happened and the way she hugged me, holding me for what felt like five whole minutes. This quiet act of kindness reached a part of me that was still hurting after the assault. It lifted a weight off my shoulders. Sometimes, a hug is all we need.

For the first time in a while, I felt seen, heard, and not judged.

She gently helped me to my feet and asked if I would like to join her for the rest of her rounds and go to her room afterward. I wiped away my tears and gave a simple nod. Before we continued, we stopped to inform the other resident assistant about the situation. As we crossed the outdoor quad toward her residence hall, the crisp night air felt like heaven. I stayed in her room through an episode of *Teen Mom*. We didn't say much, but her presence spoke volumes. She didn't ask questions or push me to talk; she simply made a space for me to feel safe. A space for a handicapped, imperfect freshman, something I yearned for but never really knew how to ask for.

The next morning, I found the strength to reach out to a family member for guidance. I knew it couldn't be Samantha or my father because my heart couldn't bear the thought of burdening or disappointing them. Think about that . . . the two people I trusted the most in my life, and I was apprehensive about disappointing them. My mission was to make them proud and to hold on to my sense of self, no matter how messy things got. I knew Samantha and my dad wouldn't take the news well; hearing about my assault or how I was spiraling would have hurt them deeply, and I wasn't ready to face that.

I decided to reach out to one of my older sisters, believing that even though she was out of state, she would be there for me. She listened with empathy, stunned into silence, then lightened the moment with her usual sarcastic humor, making me laugh through tears. Telling her about my assault brought some relief, but I couldn't help feeling let down and wanting more. I had hoped she would have dropped everything and been on the next flight to be by my side and fight this battle with me. I needed her to come tell me in person that I shouldn't allow this debilitating incident to define or destroy me— perhaps that was wishful thinking. Sadly, she never did show up, and she never mentioned it again.

This served as another reminder that this imperfect girl was most often alone in this world. I could only rely on me, myself, and I to fight and survive. The amount of heartbreak my heart has endured is beyond words.

The resident director was informed of the assault because I had confided in the resident assistant. I met with her, explained what had happened, shared Scotty's information, and she walked me through my options. In my head, I heard fictional Caption Benson's disappointed voice, saying I had washed away all the evidence, making it a challenging case to win. For my mental health, I had to evaluate if it was worth reliving the assault in greater detail and also putting my family through the strain of an investigation. I decided to give myself time to think about it from all angles. A few weeks later, the resident director called to inform me Scotty was planning to transfer to another institution at the end of the academic year. She shared this news gently, hoping it might help me decide whether to pursue an investigation or allow his future departure to offer a measure of relief.

The decision seemed clear to me: for my survival, I merely needed to steer clear of Scotty for the remainder of the school year, which is exactly what I did. I kept my head down, avoided him, achieved good grades, and still drank occasionally, but less frequently. I found a small group of friends to provide a distraction and help get me through the remainder of the year. Although I chose not to endure the pain of legal action, I now wish that those I confided in had encouraged me to seek counseling.

I'm still not entirely sure how I pulled it off, but I managed to juggle my personal struggles while earning a spot on the Dean's List both semesters. I suffered in silence, but somehow found a way to maintain balance. The hardest part of that silence was contending with the relentless voice in my head, always running, never resting and impossible to shut off. The resident director's words, "Always remember, you are a survivor," will forever be with me.

I believe that I chose the cowardly high road, and I hope you possess a stronger will than I did. If you were or are the victim of a traumatic situation, I hope you pursued the justice you deserve. In life, there are always those moments of regret, when we wish we could go back in time and re-write a piece of our story. If I could go back with my rejuvenated strength and what I know now, I would fight for my justice, in hopes that boys like Scotty never underestimate the power of an imperfect nobody again. To make him realize he is a MONSTER. I pray each day that no other women fell victim to Scotty, and if they did, they found the courage and strength to seek justice.

It's remarkable how much of my mental resilience was tested in the first quarter of my life. Perhaps my mental strength is my secret superpower.

Hang in there, the imperfect
you. Remember, NO is a
complete sentence.
Survivors will prosper no
matter how deep the wound
is; this scar is only a small
piece of my puzzle.

Use the space below to let your thoughts flow freely.

Have you ever experienced personal injustice?

Did you rely on others to assist you? Are you still seeking justice?

In your life lessons, do you feel you can help somebody in need?

Consider offering acts of kindness, such as being a supportive resource for therapy, practicing attentive listening, and creating a safe, welcoming space for others to open up.

How do you push back against someone who won't let go of the same issue and keeps ignoring your boundaries?

Remember, NO is a complete sentence.

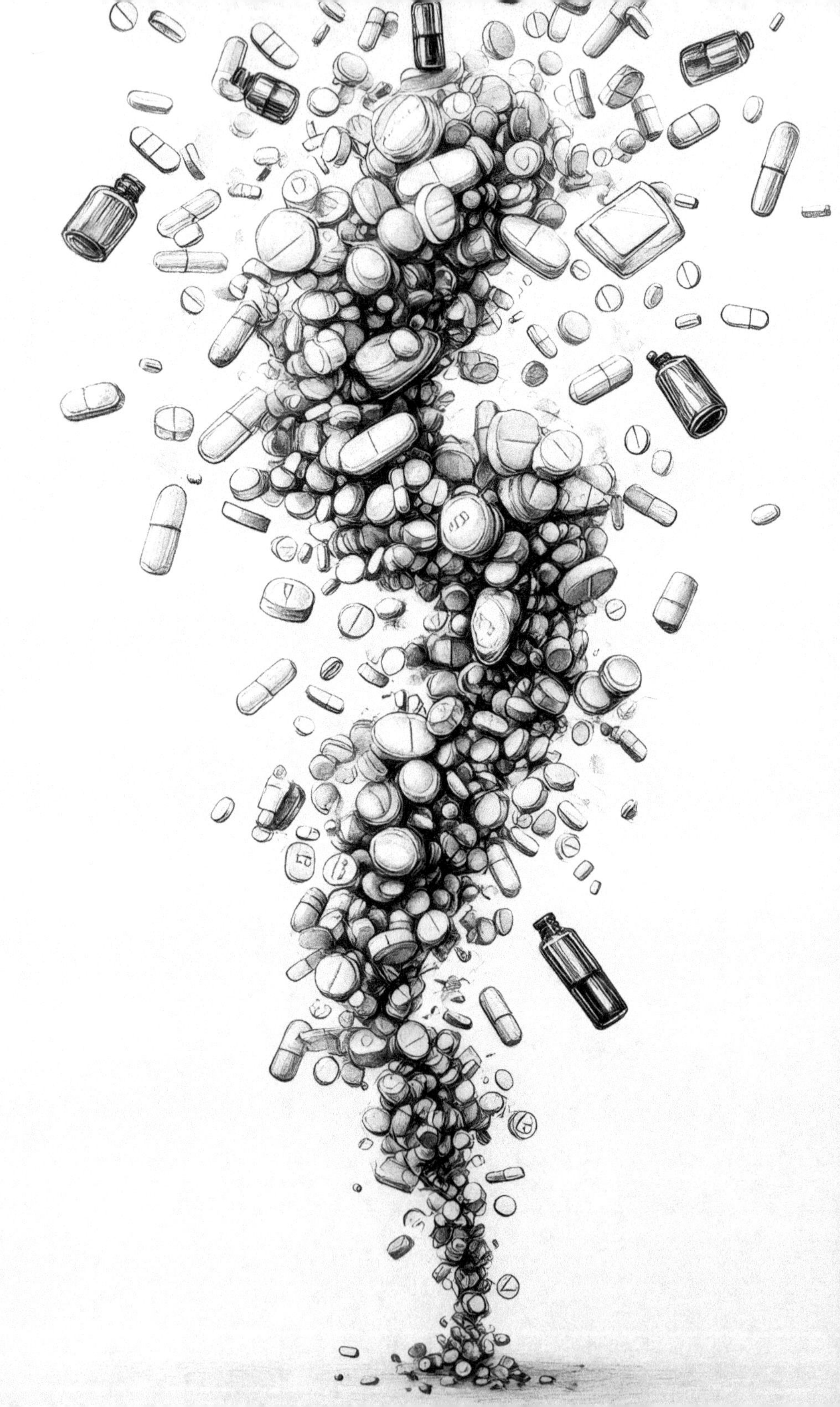

WEATHERING THE STORM

The summer of 2015 will forever remain etched in my memory. It was a season of triumph, but also held one of the hardest lessons life had to teach me. I graduated with my bachelor's degree, earning the highest academic distinction, Summa Cum Laude with a 3.8 GPA. Then instead of stopping there, I chose to stay an additional year to pursue the unthinkable, a master's degree with another 3.8 GPA. A personal, unbelievable achievement that was nothing short of extraordinary. An accomplishment that the high school imperfect me, who struggled with a 1.8 GPA, never thought was conceivable. I was told I couldn't do it. I was made to feel inadequate.

I silenced and proved all my doubters wrong.

I had built unstoppable momentum, determined to shape a future worthy of the remarkable strides I had made. But fate had other plans. My devotion was tested once again by God. Hadn't I already dealt with enough trials and tribulations?

* * *

It was a few weeks after I graduated with my master's degree that I began experiencing lower abdominal pain. The pain I was confronted with was unfamiliar and kept intensifying until it became intolerable. I made an appointment with the doctor's office. I don't remember exactly how events unraveled, but I was transitioning from pediatric to adult medicine and I made the mistake of scheduling with a male physician. If your first inkling was assuming that the male doctor said it was my monthly period . . .

Ding, Ding, Ding!

"Are you sure it's not your menstrual cycle? What you're describing sounds like typical cramps."

I thought to myself, *Yes doctor, I'm hunched over in agony because of my cramps, and I paid a co-payment for you to tell me that.*

The doctor spent ten minutes diagnosing me with "typical cramps" and told me to take over the counter ibuprofen.

Ladies, why do we believe men understand the function of a woman's anatomy?

My symptoms showed no sign of improvement, and my monthly gift never arrived. I followed up with my doctor's office, and they recommended I consult with an OB/GYN, who would hopefully offer a more accurate diagnosis than "typical cramps."

I scheduled an appointment with a female OB/GYN for a more thorough evaluation. She was attentive, listened carefully, and did not jump to conclusions about my menstrual cycle being the root cause. To investigate and better understand the source of my pelvic pain, she ordered an ultrasound, which revealed a cyst on my left ovary. The doctor outlined two possible outcomes: The cyst might resolve on its own, or, in the worst-case scenario, I would have to undergo minimal invasive surgery to have it removed. She continued to explain that ovarian cysts are common and a normal part of the reproductive cycle. She believed the cyst would resolve on its own, but prescribed Naproxen to help with the unusual amount of pelvic pain.

In the coming days, it became evident that the Naproxen wasn't potent enough. The intensity of my pain and discomfort became worse. It seemed as if my ovarian cyst had a mind of its own. It was a long process of trial and error with various narcotics to find the correct one to alleviate my pain.

Naproxen.

Tramadol.

Oxycodone-Acetaminophen.

Hydrocodone-Acetaminophen.

Dilaudid (Hydromorphone).

When I was prescribed Dilaudid, my pain was decimated, and my life was transformed. It was the first time in my life where I felt absolutely nothing at all.

I didn't *hear* people's comments. I didn't *feel* their stares. I didn't *see* them pointing. The infiltration of narcotics seizes your mental state. The sensation defies description because it is a serene feeling that overtakes your mind. I felt as if I were a caterpillar in a secure, silky cocoon with no worries or external thoughts, aiming to emerge as a beautiful butterfly. It seemed my aspiration to be someone else was coming to fruition.

The imperfect me was nonexistent.

I followed the prescription instructions carefully at the beginning of treatment, doing everything I could to manage my pain responsibly. However, my cyst didn't resolve on its own, and after enduring weeks of relentless pelvic pain, I had no choice but to have it surgically removed. The procedure itself was successful, but the aftermath took an unexpected and devastating turn. No one could have predicted that my recovery would lead me down a dark path of addiction. In many ways, the recovery process proved to be far more agonizing than the pain before it.

My procedure was considered minimally invasive, so staying overnight for further observation or additional treatment wasn't an option. Even today, my mother regrets not speaking up to keep me in the hospital. She once said, "I wish I hadn't let them discharge you. You couldn't even stand up on your own. You were sedated and unstable. You should have stayed overnight." She still laughs fondly as she recalls the priceless look of sheer horror on my face as she explained that she and the nurse had to dress me.

My mom reflects on the day of my procedure as one of the most nerve-racking and difficult experiences she's ever faced as a mother. She had no premonition of the behaviors I would exhibit at home while under the influence of potent narcotics and anesthesia. She still remembers how the anesthesiologist administered the incorrect dose, basing it on my weight that included my prosthetics instead of my actual body weight without them. To make matters worse, my addiction compelled me to secretly take a few Dilaudid before the procedure. The combination of anesthesia and Dilaudid had the potential to be lethal.

So, when the nurse casually advised, "She's good to go. You can take her home," my parents were stunned. I was heavily over-medicated, deeply sedated, and barely coherent. Years later, my mother told me it's a miracle I survived at all.

I have little memory of the day I underwent my procedure, but my mother stated it was a nightmare. She recalls that when we returned home, I wandered through the house in a daze, carefully taking down every family portrait and wrapping them in a blanket in my bedroom. I would become extremely emotional and begin to sob when seeing any pictures of Samantha.

While I was in this delirious condition, my mother heard me state, "You're not even my real parents." When she told me that, I was shocked that such a harsh and unnecessary statement had come from my own lips. To this day, I still grapple with the weight of that moment, trying to process how injurious it was for my parents to hear. I remind myself that my mind was clouded by prescription drugs, but the guilt lingers. Coming to terms with the possibility that you've hurt your loved ones is a bitter pill to swallow. It's a feeling I know all too well, having been the recipient of my mother's drug-induced harsh words wishing I would be hit by a car when I was a teen.

The hard part of hearing gut-wrenching remarks is you never know if they are someone's genuine truth; you know, the kind of truth someone expresses after having one too many drinks. No one is perfect. Words can sting. My parents and I have learned to reflect on my procedure day with a sense of humor, finding ways to laugh amid chaos. It taught us valuable lessons about how to navigate any possible future circumstances.

* * *

The day after my procedure, I returned to the hospital in excruciating pain. They administered morphine intravenously, but it didn't offer any relief. I was admitted, and they switched to injecting hydromorphone into my veins. The best *worst* high of my life! A turning point from which there was no return. I was placed in a wonderful, private room on the maternity floor, widely regarded as the most comfortable floor in the hospital. It was staffed by the kindest and most attentive nurses. I had a few Dilaudid pills tucked in my pocket, as I never left the house without them. I took a couple before the nurse began setting up my hydromorphone IV. As you might imagine, the rest of the day was a bit of a blur because I was higher than the sky. However, I distinctly remember the nurse asking what I would like for dinner. I requested a peanut butter and banana sandwich. She smiled and told me it was not on the menu, but she would check with the kitchen to see if they could accommodate my request. Ultimately, the hospital kitchen staff came through with my gourmet sandwich request. *Mmm* . . . there was nothing like my routine scrumptious peanut butter and banana sandwich to keep me company during my stay.

I spent a few days in the hospital feeling like royalty with the intravenous hydromorphone coursing through my veins. I gazed out the window, refueled my soul with different genres of music, and savored my delicious sandwiches. It was the calmest I have ever felt.

No anxiety.

No responsibility.

No internalizing hurtful comments.

No stares.

No pain . . . just bliss.

I truly believed the opioids were helping me, even though they were causing false euphoria—the simplicity of tranquility. My perception was askew.

No one came to visit me, but I wasn't surprised. I had spent my entire life navigating solitude, so why would this situation be any different.

I responded well to the treatment, and my pain remained at a manageable level. I was discharged from the hospital feeling like ice had replaced my blood. I felt cold and distant, unsure of who I was. The attending physician prescribed a fresh new bottle of Dilaudid. I now had two full prescription bottles in my possession, in addition to the pills I already had at home. I had so many pills to keep me high.

As far as the physician supplying me with so much . . . the left hand didn't know what the right hand was doing.

My paranoia took over. I knew it was imperative for me to hide my pills from my mother at all costs. I was uncertain about what she took to render herself incapacitated, I just knew I couldn't risk her getting near my only source of serenity and freedom. I stashed bottles in various places in my bedroom—one beneath my mattress, another in a drawer, and a third tucked inside a shoe in my closet. During the haze of my high, panic would strike. I'd forget where I'd hidden all my pills and would tear apart my room in a frenzy until I found a bottle.

I realized I had a problem when the instructions on the medicine bottle no longer mattered. I would simply pop a pill whenever I needed to take the edge off. It became difficult to distinguish genuine physical pain from the illusions my mind conjured, convincing me I was hurting even when I wasn't. Whenever I had an appointment, my OB/GYN would shake her head, baffled and visibly frustrated. She couldn't understand why my recovery seemed more painful than the chronic pelvic pain I endured before surgery. In a cruel twist, I had traded one form of suffering for another: the persistent ache of recovery replaced my tormented cyst pain I thought I was escaping.

My addiction had me in and out of the hospital almost every other week that summer. I would be given my hydromorphone IV high, my gourmet peanut butter and banana sandwich, a new bottle of narcotics, and be discharged. My suffering became so severe that a family friend gave me extra Oxycodone-Acetaminophen to help alleviate my pain.

In retrospect, it's eerie how opioids manipulated my mind to satisfy my craving to be high. Looking back, I find it hard to believe I functioned at all. I popped my painkillers as if they were candy, causing the summer of 2015 to be nonexistent.

One afternoon, as I sat on the couch, the weight of reality began to press down on me. I took a handful of pills over the course of an hour. Desperate for relief, I called my OB/GYN during her shift at the hospital to complain about my pain. Her voice was grated with frustration as she put her foot down and firmly said, "Kat, I can tell you are high right now. You need to stop taking the Dilaudid. I cannot have a conversation with you while you are high."

I hung up the phone, and my first inclination was to take another pill. *Who is she to judge me?* I stumbled to my bedroom and rummaged to find a bottle of my pills. I found a bottle but could barely read the label with my blurred vision. I sat on the edge of my bed, head tilted, rubbing my forehead with my left hand, trying to get hold of myself. In my right hand, the prescription bottle rattled softly as I rocked back and forth. I contemplated my life. *What is happening to me? Who am I turning into? How did I get here?* It finally dawned on me that I was addicted to painkillers.

The following scene played out like a movie I never wanted to star in. It was a moment so stark it shattered my denial and drove me to sobriety. I was scared, strung out, and desperate for help. My mother was in the kitchen at the stove, cooking in a fog, intoxicated by whatever pills she'd taken that day. Her movements were slow and detached. I watched her from the counter, leaning against its edge, facing her left side.

In a trembling tone I said, "Mom, I think I'm addicted to my painkillers, and I'm not sure what to do."

She turned her head slowly, her glassy eyes struggling to focus. Wiping her dry mouth she mumbled, "Yeah, well what are you going to do. It happens."

Damn.

Her words in this moment struck me like a freight train.

I was dumbfounded.

I was speechless.

I was hurt.

This was the vital wake-up call I hadn't known I needed. It felt like a portion of my soul had died. I sobered up right away.

My own mother had no compassion or drive to assist me in overcoming my addiction to narcotics. How dare she! My own mother! She was content with her own daughter deteriorating at home, popping pills just like her . . . *the irony.*

As I reflect, I recognize that I shouldn't have been surprised; how could I expect my sick mother to help me when she was incapable of helping herself? It was wishful thinking that her maternal instincts would have sprung into high gear.

I immediately stopped taking all narcotics. *It was awful!*

If you want a harsh taste of reality, try going cold turkey off opioids. It's like whiplash. I was unaware that you need to gradually taper off because quitting cold turkey puts your immune system into shock. I had unpleasant and painful withdrawals. My body shut down.

I couldn't lay down or sleep.

I couldn't eat or drink. It felt like my esophagus was clogged.

I couldn't use the bathroom. My system was dried up.

I walked hunched over, shaking and shuffling my feet.

I called my dad who was house-sitting for my older sister to take me to the hospital because I wasn't sure if I would live another day. As my life flashed before my eyes, I questioned: "God, didn't I do the right thing? I stopped taking my painkillers. Why are you punishing me?"

My dad took me to the emergency room, where the doctor confirmed I was experiencing severe withdrawal symptoms. They administered IV fluids, but my immune system was in turmoil, adjusting to the absence of the deadly narcotics it had come to depend on. I just had to weather the storm . . .

It took three weeks of weathering the storm for my body to start functioning in a normal capacity again. Exhausted and sleep deprived, I spent most of my time propped up in my darkened bedroom, surrounded by a fortress of pillows that gave me some sense of comfort. Damn, what a season to reflect on! I still can't quite grasp how I made it through that hellish, drug-fueled, relentless, self-destructive summer. It tested every part of me, and somehow, I am still standing. I thank God for watching over me and helping me once again to ignite my mental resilience.

That summer served as another reminder that I was an imperfect girl alone in the world. I could only rely on me, myself, and I to fight and survive. I'm repeating myself, but it was a regular occurrence in my life. Regardless of where my life takes me, I will always bet on myself. That alone is worth its weight in gold. I will always be my loudest cheerleader, rooting for myself, no matter what!

It's important to recognize that saving those who seek comfort in their own brokenness is not always possible. Not all individuals want to be saved. Instead, you must make the tough choice to save yourself. Prioritize your own needs.

Hang in there, the imperfect you. You possess greater resilience than you realize. Sometimes, it's just a matter of understanding your own mental strength and fortitude.

Use the space below to let your thoughts flow freely.

What is the toughest challenge you have overcome?

Did you realize your own failure, or did someone else alert you of it?

Did you ever feel dismissed when you were in need?

Have you ever asked for help and you were turned down or given poor advice?

When was the last time you took a guiltless day just to pamper yourself and reset?

How did it feel to be refreshed? If you haven't, would you consider making time for you?

ON THE BRINK OF TOMORROW

My life is not a movie. But if it were, this would be where the camera gently pans past a bright white picket fence, tulips swaying in the breeze, and sunlight spilling across the freshly cut lawn. I would be jogging toward what would seem like my happily ever after. However, this is not a cinematic fairytale. It is my life story to this day. There is so much of my life to still unravel, explore, and write. I've faced more obstacles and adversities than I could fit between two covers. There is only so much a heart can bear and only so many tears that can be shed before the ink starts to blur. My battles are still unfolding, and I plan to continue to share my journey with you when the time is right.

For a long time, I felt as if I lived on the sidelines in the shadow of my own life. Does that sound crazy to you? I have always waited silently and faded into the background. And what was the result? My invisibility allowed me to quietly build, brick by brick, my own success. I laid the foundation of a life that is mine. Not gifted. Not inherited. Tirelessly earned. *Everything I have is because of me.*

I am blessed beyond words, but that doesn't mean it was easy. What is easy in life? It's the small things that tend to be overlooked. I have built my own self-worth and net worth. I own my home and share it with two beautiful dogs who remind me daily what true, authentic, unconditional love looks and feels like. I safeguard my serenity, speak sparingly, and keep a close-knit circle reserved for those who've earned my trust. I have a job that I genuinely enjoy, and I don't take it for granted, knowing this isn't the case for everyone.

As we mature, we recognize a common thread—every generation aspires to be better off than their parents. But adulthood comes without a manual, leaving us to navigate through choices we must ultimately live with. My choice is to rewrite and craft a better narrative because it is never too late. My goal is to be successful, live without financial fear, feel proud of who I am, and not be defined by what I have survived. I intend to embody and prove this truth in my upcoming chapters ahead, and I hope you feel inspired to do the same.

After the summer when I saved myself from what could have been a detrimental opioid addiction, I found myself on the brink of a new beginning. I obtained my first real job in the big city. At that time, my father had moved back in with my mother, and my initial plan was to live at home with them for a year to save money—but of course, that didn't work out. What else is new? They lived in subsidized housing, and because my income would have raised their rent, they asked me to contribute toward the roof over my head. Contributing financially to a space that felt toxic was something I simply could not accept. Instead, I used whatever I had in savings to rent a condo across from a train station, so I could commute to work independently. I also picked up a second job to pay off the private college loan my aunt and uncle co-signed for me. I'm not someone who likes to owe anyone, so I hustled seven days a week with no breaks. It took me only four years to repay a ten-year loan. I worked early mornings, late nights, and missed social gatherings, but it was worth it! It meant everything to me and carried even greater meaning to my aunt, as it fulfilled my promise to her. They took a chance on me—something I will forever be grateful for and never take lightly. Without them, who knows where I would be today.

Samantha, my closest ally and sister, found a boyfriend through one of those online dating sites and eventually moved down south with his family. Today, she is a proud and exceptional mother to the most beautiful little boy who is a spitting image of her. I wish we lived closer so we could share countless waking moments together. I know without a doubt we would spend every holiday at each other's homes and practically be inseparable. Fortunately, distance has never dimmed our bond. She is always a phone call away—still my protector and unfailingly reminding me how proud she is of me. Regardless of how much time has passed, we effortlessly pick up right where we left off. Samantha will forever and always be my ray of sunshine on even the cloudiest days.

My father is still the quintessential salesman chasing that elusive dollar that never quite materializes. A few years ago, he gave us all a scare when he was diagnosed with a rare viral throat cancer. It was the first time fear hit harder than heartbreak because I couldn't fathom the possibility of losing my lifelong constant. Each hospital visit left me in tears at his bedside. I know strength is expected when visiting someone ill, but when it comes to my dad, I can never hold it together. I silently prayed for just one more day each visit. I wasn't ready to say goodbye. I know, no one ever really is. I needed more time to make him proud, even if it frequently feels unattainable. By the grace of God and the incredible team at the Veterans Health Administration Hospital (VA), he pulled through. He is still with us today. Our relationship has evolved, and we equally make the effort to call one another. Together, we go out to eat and exercise at his preferred gym.

Don't worry, he still lives and breathes golf. As one of my sisters likes to jokingly say, "Take that to the golf course, Dad." If he's not at a sales meeting or at the VA, you will certainly find him playing nine holes or hitting a bucket of balls.

My mother's addictive tendencies are woven into a fabric of who she is and will forever be an undeniable part of her story. I am one of the few in my family who choose to have a relationship with her. In my eyes, you only get one mother in this life, and if you are lucky, one who rescues you, so I don't overlook the significance of that. She has come a long way. The relationship we share now is something I never imagined would be possible. When I find myself drowning in the weight of it all some days, she is that one call. I give my mother credit—she is surprisingly good at talking me down from a ledge and easing my anxiety. In those rare, fleeting moments, her motherly instincts surface, tender and real, a glimpse of what was so often absent during my childhood. In return, I am her sounding board too, an ear to listen when the world feels cruel. I try to guide her toward light when her thoughts spiral into darkness. I try to provide positive reinforcement and remind her she shouldn't allow thoughts that will set her back to consume her. Many have turned away from her and written her off. Friends, my siblings, and other relatives are unable and unwilling to forgive her for the many past transgressions they experienced. I try to see both sides. At times, it's hard for me to witness, even as I remember the amount of pain she has caused me and others. However, I wholeheartedly believe having a mental health illness doesn't make her a terrible person. My mother and I both carry the ache of abandonment; perhaps that is why I cannot turn the other way. Is my mother perfect? No, but who the hell is?

So here I am, after the grand circus of life has unfolded—drumroll, please. The suspense is unbearable, isn't it? The nail-biting question: Where am I now? Well—I'm still standing. I am a self-sufficient woman, still growing from every lesson, uncovering new strengths from within, learning to love myself, and in that love, thriving. I am not who I used to be. I have become someone stronger, wiser, and more whole. As my story continues to be written, those around me tell me to reflect and give myself grace. I've been told time after time that I don't allow myself the moments of contentment I have earned and deserve. I need to learn to celebrate the haves, release the have nots. As I mentioned at the start of this book, it is important for me to find joy in all the victories, big and small, in my life, just like HER. I'm not sure if my relentless pursuit of perfection will ever allow me to give myself grace because I live in a never-be-satisfied mindset. Let's pray I learn to live in the moment.

In a world that has never made room for me, I aspire to continue my life's journey with the desire to be better and stronger than ever in my daily walk toward acceptance. I'll persevere in my quest to find the meaning behind each of God's obstacles and store them away until I need to apply them in my life's voyage.

* * *

To The Imperfect You,

I hope that by sharing my life experiences, I can inspire, motivate, and connect with you as you navigate your own journey toward acceptance. May the lessons I've learned and the insights I've gained serve as meaningful guideposts you carry with you along the way. Hold on to some of the key takeaways:

Find someone like HER to look up to; the one person who provides you with courage and confidence to persevere.

Don't let societal stares, pointing, and debilitating comments define or destroy you.

Dismiss those everyday microaggressions.

Never let your trauma define you. Rather, let it define your strength.

Find your wins in life no matter how big or small. Only you will know when you achieve them.

Discover your superpower. Mine was my mental resilience.

Most importantly, use your scars and agony to remind yourself that you are a survivor and a fighter. Regardless of your life's journey, bet on yourself, because that's worth its weight in gold. Your disabilities don't have to define your capabilities.

Hang in there,
the imperfect you.
As your story continues
to be written, ask yourself
how you want to be
remembered. May our paths
cross again as our journeys
continue to unfold.

From one imperfect person
to another... your beauty is
deeper than the surface,
so be kind to yourself.

Use the space below to let your thoughts flow freely.

Are there any key takeaways or lessons that resonated with you?

They can be positive or negative. How did they change your thought process?

What does success look like to you right now?

Has your definition of success changed over time? What matters most to you today?

What does your walk toward acceptance look like?

Is it for society, school, work, or yourself? The walk could be big or small, long or short. Just know you will get there. I have faith in you!

ACKNOWLEDGEMENTS

If you had told the younger imperfect me who struggled with reading comprehension that I would one day become an author, I would have laughed in disbelief. Writing my life's story has been an emotional roller coaster. I'm especially thankful to the few individuals who inspired me to share my story.

Through countless heartfelt conversations, Mima, my extraordinary neighbor, friend, and nurturing mother figure with a heart of gold, was instrumental in making my book a reality.

I am thankful to HER for inspiring me to share my story with the hope of it resonating with others as they strive to discover their own light and become the most desirable, empowered, and authentic versions of themselves.

I am deeply grateful for the constant love and unwavering support my dad and Samantha give me every day. I hope to keep making you both proud.

Last but not least, I offer a flower to my mother, who continues striving to make amends with those around her.

ABOUT THE AUTHOR

Kat Floridia obtained her Bachelor of Science degree in Business Administration, Master of Science degree in Organizational Leadership, and Graduate Certificate in Healthcare Management with the highest academic distinction. She has been the driving force behind  her own professional success, continually striving to become the best version of herself. Kat is committed to empowering others by sharing her story—one shaped by resilience, growth, and the lessons found in life's most challenging moments. She finds joy in loving her two dogs, following professional basketball, and drawing strength from the women who inspire her. Her quiet acts of selflessness remain a steady presence in her life, especially for those who look to her as their guiding light.

www.ingramcontent.com/pod-product-compliance
Lightning Source LLC
Chambersburg PA
CBHW070521160726
48003CB00004B/1657